The
Future
of
American
Intelligence

*This book is a publication
of the Hoover Institution's*

**Initiative
on**
*National Priorities,
International Rivalries,
and Global Cooperation*

*The Hoover Institution
gratefully acknowledges
the generous support of*

JERONIMO *and* JAVIER ARANGO

THE LYNDE AND HARRY BRADLEY FOUNDATION

on this publication.

The Future of American Intelligence

Edited by
Peter Berkowitz

HOOVER INSTITUTION PRESS
Stanford University   Stanford, California

www.hoover.org

Hoover Institution Press Publication No. 540

First printing, 2005
12 11 10 09 08 07 06 05   9 8 7 6 5 4 3 2 1

Manufactured in the United States of America

The paper used in this publication meets the minimum requirements
of the American National Standard for Information Sciences—
Permanence of Paper for Printed Library Materials, ANSI Z39.48-1992. ⊚

Library of Congress Cataloging-in-Publication Data
The future of American intelligence / edited by Peter Berkowitz.
      p.   cm. — (Hoover Institution Press publication ; no. 540)
   Includes bibliographical references and index.
   ISBN 0-8179-4662-4 (alk. paper)
   1. Intelligence service—United States.   2. National security—United
States.   3. Terrorism—United States—Prevention.   I. Berkowitz, Peter,
1959–   II. Series: Hoover Institution Press publication ; 540.
JK468.I6F88   2005
327.1273—dc22   2005016688

Contents

Acknowledgments

Bruce Berkowitz (no relation) provided advice on the structure of this book and encouragement in bringing the many pieces of the intelligence reform puzzle together. As always, Hoover Institution director John Raisian and deputy director Dave Brady have provided generous resources for the study of American ideas and institutions.

Peter Berkowitz
Washington, DC

Contributors

Peter Berkowitz teaches at George Mason University School of Law and is the Tad and Dianne Taube Research Fellow at the Hoover Institution, Stanford University. He is cofounder and director of the Israel Program on Constitutional Government and served as a senior consultant to the President's Council on Bioethics. He is the author of *Virtue and the Making of Modern Liberalism* (Princeton University Press) and *Nietzsche: The Ethics of an Immoralist* (Harvard University Press), as well as editor of *Terrorism, the Laws of War, and the Constitution: Debating the Enemy Combatant Cases* (Hoover Institution Press), *Varieties of Progressivism in America* (Hoover Institution Press), *Varieties of Conservatism in America* (Hoover Institution Press), and *Never a Matter of Indifference: Sustaining Virtue in a Free Republic* (Hoover Institution Press). He has written on a variety of topics for a variety of publications.

Reuel Marc Gerecht is a resident fellow at the American Enterprise

Institute. He is also a contributing editor at the *Weekly Standard* and a correspondent for the *Atlantic Monthly*. From 1985 to 1994, Mr. Gerecht served in the CIA's Clandestine Service, where he specialized in Middle Eastern affairs. He is the author of *Know Thine Enemy: A Spy's Journey into Revolutionary Iran* (Farrar, Straus, and Giroux) and of *The Islamic Paradox: Shi'ite Clerics, Sunni Fundamentalists, and the Coming of Arab Democracy* (AEI Press).

Gordon Nathaniel Lederman served on the 9/11 Commission's staff and was responsible for issues related to intelligence reform. He is the author of *Reorganizing the Joint Chiefs of Staff: The Goldwater-Nichols Department of Defense Reorganization Act of 1986* and several other publications. He was an associate in the National Security Law and Policy Group at the law firm of Arnold & Porter and is a magna cum laude graduate of Harvard College and Harvard Law School.

Kevin M. O'Connell is the director of the Washington-based Center for Intelligence Research and Analysis, which performs research and analysis for people and organizations involved in U.S. intelligence. A twenty-year veteran of U.S. intelligence, Mr. O'Connell was formerly the director of RAND's Intelligence Policy Center and has held positions in the Office of the Vice President; on the National Security Council; and in the office of the Director of Central Intelligence, Community Management Staff. He has served on a number of high-level boards, including the National Geospatial Intelligence Advisory Board, a Defense Advanced Research Pojects Agency–NGA panel, and the Director of Homeland Security Information Policy Board. He also served as the staff director of the National Imagery and Mapping Agency Commission. Mr. O'Connell is an adjunct professor of security studies at Georgetown University and has taught intelligence policy in the RAND Graduate School.

Gary J. Schmitt is executive director of the Project for the New American Century, a Washington-based think tank. A former minority staff director of the Senate Select Committee on Intelligence and former executive director of the President's Foreign Intelligence Advisory Board, Dr. Schmitt is the coauthor, with Abram N. Shulsky, of *Silent Warfare: Understanding the World of Intelligence* (3rd edition).

Richard H. Shultz Jr. is the director of the International Security Studies Program at the Fletcher School of Law and Diplomacy and a professor of international politics. He is also director of research for the Consortium for the Study of Intelligence in Washington, DC. He has written extensively on intelligence and security. His recent books and articles include *The Secret War Against Hanoi: Kennedy and Johnson's Use of Spies, Saboteurs, and Covert Warriors in North Vietnam* (1999; paperback 2000); *Security Studies for the 21st Century* (coeditor and author; 1997); "Showstoppers: Nine Reasons Why We Never Sent Our Special Operations Forces After al Qaeda Before 9/11," *The Weekly Standard* (Jan. 26, 2004); and "It's War: Fighting Post-11 September Global Terrorism Through a Doctrine of Preemption," *Terrorism and Political Violence* (Spring 2003). He has also served as a consultant to U.S. government agencies concerned with national security affairs.

Introduction

Peter Berkowitz

ONCE THE PROVINCE of policy wonks of the most esoteric variety, intelligence reform since the surprise attacks of 9/11 has galvanized public attention. The failure to discover weapons of mass destruction in Iraq two years later intensified the concern. To determine what went wrong and how to improve American intelligence, two blue-ribbon commissions were formed. In November 2002, Congress and the president created the National Commission on Terrorist Attacks upon the United States. Published in July 2004, *The 9/11 Commission Report* was greeted with critical acclaim and, improbably, became a national best-seller. The bulk of the report explored the rise of Islamic extremism and the new threat posed to American national security by the deadly forms of terrorism al Qaeda and its ilk had developed. In conclusion, the report made a series of proposals for restructuring the U.S. intelligence services. Scarcely four months later, after a bitterly fought presidential election and with little examination of the merits of the 9/11 Commission's proposals, Congress passed, and President George W. Bush signed into law on December 17, 2004, the Intelligence Reform and Terrorism Prevention Act of 2004, which largely enacted the commission's recommendations.

Meanwhile, in February 2004, while the 9/11 Commission was in the midst of its work, the president created the Commission on the Intelligence Capabilities of the United States Regarding Weapons of Mass Destruction. The WMD Commission, which presented its report to the public on March 31, 2005, concluded that U.S. intelligence about Iraqi WMD was "dead wrong"; current U.S. intelligence about the nuclear capabilities of other countries is poor; the nation's intelligence collection and analysis rely on outmoded assumptions that rigidified during the Cold War and that thwart proper analysis of today's adversaries; and the intelligence community suffers from a sclerotic bureaucratic structure that stifles creative thinking and independent judgment. In short, debate about the future of American intelligence—including questions about the effectiveness of the recent restructuring itself—has only just begun.

The essays gathered in this volume refine the debate. They deepen understanding of the new national security threats presented by terrorism, by the proliferation of weapons of mass destruction, and by the spread of Islamic extremism. They bring into focus the variety of obstacles—intellectual, governmental, bureaucratic, military, and technological—to making U.S. intelligence more capable of gathering effectively, interpreting accurately, and conveying concisely to policy makers knowledge about our new adversaries. They also put forward recommendations for effective reform. Distinguished and diverse, the contributors approach the problem from a variety of disciplinary perspectives. Yet whether from the perspective of the political scientist, policy analyst, lawyer, or journalist, they converge in arguing that the task of reforming U.S. intelligence is urgent, the challenges are formidable, and the stakes are high.

Richard Shultz opens the volume by exploring the rise and nature of nonstate armed groups and the distinctive features of the national security threat they pose. Until September 11, the United States, in accordance with the conventional wisdom, viewed other states as the major threat to national security. However, the massive terrorist assault on American soil threw into sharp relief the capacity of nonstate armed groups to strike high-value strategic targets through asymmetric means not only in the United States but across the globe. Indeed, armed groups have emerged as major players capable of undermining states and provoking regional instability in ways that directly affect America's vital national security interests.

The international context in which armed groups have emerged, stresses Shultz, is characterized by a crucial paradox. Even as globalization has promoted integration through the creation of international markets, the development of regional and transnational cooperation, and the spread of liberal and democratic norms, it has also contributed to the alarming rise of failed states, which in turn has produced serious fragmentation in the international order and has left lawless and ungoverned areas where armed groups can find safe haven. Although they differ in crucial respects, the power of all these nonstate actors has grown dramatically since World War II, and all have taken advantage of the information-age technology and network-based approaches to organization encouraged by globalization. By distinguishing the variety of armed groups—insurgents, terrorists, militias, and criminal organizations—Shultz seeks to bring into focus the peculiar threat they represent, as well as the need for the intelligence community to refashion intellectual tools that were designed to combat the specific threats posed by nation-states.

Gary Schmitt argues that one of the main reasons the U.S. intelligence community failed to come to grips with "the novelty and the gravity of the threat posed by" one particular armed group, that of bin Laden, was their deeply entrenched assumptions and ideas about how to collect and analyze intelligence. The dominant view, dating back to the late 1940s and the creation of the CIA, is that intelligence differs from policy making and should be kept strictly separate from it because it involves applying the methods of value-neutral social science. In Schmitt's view, the demand for value neutrality is overdrawn and has bad consequences. Because hard facts are hard to come by and must always be given context by larger views of morals, politics, and foreign affairs, intelligence analysis can never, without becoming trivial or irrelevant, be separated entirely from debatable opinions, values, and policy judgments. Moreover, because intelligence is a craft and not a precise science, the United States will never be able to avoid surprise attacks altogether. The goal should be to make policy makers more deliberative.

The intelligence community should concentrate on placing new information in larger contexts and on alerting policy makers to the array of potential dangers and potential opportunities. Accordingly, Schmitt recommends lowering the "sacred curtain" between intelligence analysis and policy making by employing those trained in intelligence gathering and analysis to serve as liaisons to the policy-making world. In addition, to promote creative and critical thinking, he recommends moving from a consensus-driven National Intelligence Estimate to the production of multiple competing reports that draw on analysts from both the intelligence and the policy-making community. Schmitt worries that, unfortunately, the Intelligence Reform Act may do little to change the way analysts think about intelligence and communicate with policy makers. Indeed, he argues that the act's further centralization of intelligence in a single director and center may, if not managed carefully, actually result in the president receiving a less "accurate picture of not only what we do know but also what we don't."

Gordon Lederman shifts the focus from ideas to institutions. He

presents the case for the 9/11 Commission's major recommendations—the creation of a director of National Intelligence (DNI) to
oversee the array of intelligence operations in the United States and
the establishment of a National Counterterrorism Center to integrate intelligence on and conduct operational planning against terror—and for the Intelligence Reform Act that implemented these
recommendations. The old system, brought into existence by the
National Act of 1947, lacked a strong central management structure. In particular, it was led by the director of Central Intelligence
(DCI), who served as head of the CIA as well as head of all of the
many other intelligence operations in the country. This stretched
the DCI and exposed him to an ineliminable conflict of interest.
Moreover, the DCI lacked such routine, yet critical, executive pow-
ers as control over funding and hiring of senior managers. In contrast, the new director of National Intelligence established by the
Intelligence Reform Act does not run the CIA and is endowed with
a fuller range of executive power.

Beyond organizational structure, the old system was in need of
reform because it was designed with the Soviet threat in mind. The
Soviets could be deterred by America's nuclear capabilities, and the
conventional strikes that the Soviet Union could mount, which
required slow and obvious mobilizations, would give American
intelligence plenty of time to react. However, suicidal terrorists,
using advanced communications technology, operating around the
globe, and bent on accomplishing mass destruction, present different challenges that demand greater swiftness and efficiency. The
aim of the newly created National Counterterrorism Center, Lederman emphasizes, is to serve as the focal point for intelligence
analysis and to better coordinate intelligence acquisition, military
planning, behind-the-scenes diplomacy, public diplomacy and foreign aid, law enforcement operations, and border security.

Reuel Marc Gerecht proceeds from the hard-hitting assertion
that not only has America's Clandestine Service—responsible for

recruiting foreign agents and penetrating the enemies' organizations—not performed well against Islamic extremism, but it has
actually consistently performed poorly since the onset of the Cold
War. The principal problem is the inability of intelligence agents to
meet Islamic terrorists, or those who might associate, or even
remotely know those who might associate, with Islamic terrorists.
So what can be done to reconstruct the CIA so that it can better
target Muslim extremists? According to Gerecht, the problem runs
deep: Until the internal culture and conventional mind-set at the
CIA is cured, the Clandestine Service will remain ineffective in the
fight against bin Laden. The first step is to repudiate "the recruitment myth." Gerecht contends that the supposed Cold War golden
era—in which "inside" officers, ensconced at U.S. embassies in the
guise of staff diplomats, found new recruits through suave interaction at formal cocktail parties—was largely a fantasy. In fact, case
officers have always tended to be risk averse, careerist, and subject
to counterproductive incentives emanating from headquarters at
Langley. At this point, argues Gerecht, simple reforms won't work.
Instead, a major overhaul is needed.

To make the Clandestine Service more operationally effective,
Gerecht advises, agents abroad should be sharply reduced. He
would reconstruct the Clandestine Services around the nonofficial
cover officer (NOC), who works well beyond the walls of embassies
and the sealed world of public diplomacy. A small cadre of NOCs
in critical foreign hot spots would have many advantages where it
counts: in setting up Muslim front organizations, in getting close to
prospective Muslim agents, and in joining radical groups.

Kevin O'Connell goes beyond the specific challenges dealt with
in *The 9/11 Commission Report* and addressed by the Intelligence
Reform Act to consider how American intelligence can best take
advantage of extraordinary new developments in science and technology. While the search for better technology is as old as war, we
have entered, thanks to the information revolution, "a new intelli-

gence age" or "an era of transparency." The abundance of new information and techniques of communication does not mean, however, that the whereabouts and intentions of the enemy are now more clear. E-mail, the Internet, and global positioning systems are available to terrorists as well as to us. Certainly much can be done to improve the management of technical intelligence resources, especially in the area of intelligence collection, but the difficulties must be faced forthrightly. The main difficulty, according to O'Connell, is that even as technology makes possible the collection of more and richer data, it also requires greater education and training for it to be interpreted effectively.

Given the high cost and complexity of the technical systems involved, the director of National Intelligence will have his work cut out for him. It will be necessary to create small teams that will focus on the new technologies, to build flexibility into the budget, to recruit highly qualified people, and to encourage risk-taking, experimentation, and innovation within the intelligence community's massive bureaucracies. In addition, intelligence agencies will have to become more focused on assessment of their priorities in the collection of data, more rigorous in their management of the flow of data, more supple in their dealing with U.S. industry, and more sophisticated in their understanding of trade-offs between resources devoted to collecting data and resources devoted to analyzing it. Precisely because a consensus has emerged that U.S. intelligence services are ripe for reform, now is the moment, O'Connell stresses, to incorporate science and technology into the reform agenda.

America faces new kinds of adversaries, armed with smarter and more sinister weapons, who are capable, while dispersed around the globe, of communicating and coordinating actions with unprecedented ease. As the contributors to this volume demonstrate, this changing world requires changes in how the United States collects and analyzes intelligence and translates it into policy.

In particular, in an age of Muslim extremism and global terrorist networks, the intelligence community must revise the assumptions that underlie, and the ideas that inform, intelligence work; must reform the management style and organizational structure of the intelligence services; and must establish more effective procedures for taking advantage of the dizzying pace of technological advance. Improving the quality of the public debate about the intelligence community is a small but essential step.

1

The
Era
of
Armed
Groups

Richard H. Shultz Jr.

I. INTRODUCTION

Armed groups—terrorists, insurgents, militias, and criminal organizations—present three major challenges to the United States today. First, some groups have developed capabilities to strike high-value strategic targets across the globe through asymmetric means. Al Qaeda leveled direct strategic blows against the United States, causing a radical change in U.S. policy. Second, armed groups employ standard terrorist and insurgent tactics to attack the United States regionally to undermine U.S. policies and commitments, as the war in Iraq illustrates. Third, armed groups are major regional players who employ indirect and protracted violence to undermine the stability of states and regions where the United States has important interests at stake, such as Colombia and the Andean Ridge, Lebanon, and the Philippines.

   In addition to challenges, armed groups can also provide opportunities. In certain instances, armed groups may, if taken advantage of, contribute to the attainment of U.S. foreign policy objectives.

These challenges and opportunities need to be understood in the new context created by the end of the Cold War and the advent of globalization, which have permitted armed groups of many kinds to thrive. Unfortunately, the intelligence community, particularly the CIA—both during the Cold War and in its aftermath—has thought about and dealt with armed groups in an *episodic, transitory,* and *ad hoc* manner. Yet there is little to suggest that armed groups are a fleeting phenomenon. Rather, several trends illustrate just the opposite. Thus, the United States and its intelligence community will have to implement a variety of reforms to respond effectively to the challenges and opportunities presented by armed groups in the twenty-first century.

II. THE POST-COLD WAR SECURITY CONTEXT AND THE EVOLUTION OF ARMED GROUPS

Even before the Cold War ended, it was evident that new forces and actors were part of an evolving international security environment. Several reports and studies in the late 1990s highlighted these changes and estimated their impact on stability and conflict in the twenty-first century.[1]

1. Some examples include National Intelligence Council (NIC), *Global Trends 2015: A Dialogue About the Future with Nongovernment Experts* (December 2000); Zalmay Khalilzad and Ian O. Lesser, eds., *Sources of Conflict in the 21st Century: Regional Futures and U.S. Strategy* (Washington, DC: RAND, April 1998); Ted Robert Gurr, *Peoples Versus States: Minorities at Risk in the New Century* (Washington, DC: United States Institute of Peace, 2000); Donald L. Horowitz, *Ethnic Groups in Conflict* (Los Angeles: University of California at Berkeley, 2000); Mary Kaldor, *New and Old Wars: Organized Violence in a Global Era* (Stanford, CA: Stanford University Press, July 1999); Sudhir Kakar, *Colors of Violence: Cultural Identities, Religion, and Conflict* (Chicago: University of Chicago Press, February 1996); Charles W. Kegley Jr. and Eugene R. Wittkopf, *World Politics: Trends and Transformations*, 9th ed. (Belmont, CA: Wadsworth Press, 2004); John Bailey and Roy Godson, eds., *Organized Crime and Democratic Gov-*

A common theme running through many of these works is the need to develop a new framework or paradigm that takes into account a global environment in which the dynamics of change and the emergence of new actors have a powerful impact on the once-dominant role of states. Within this context, there is general agreement that nonstate armed groups are proliferating in number and importance. However, there is disagreement over the nature and extent of the challenge posed by these new actors.

James Rosenau's *Along the Domestic-Foreign Frontier: Exploring Governance in a Turbulent World* provides an incisive description and analytic breakdown of this new international environment.[2] It consists of the following six developments, each of which accelerated in the 1990s due to the rapid advance of information-age technology:

- Shifting and increasingly porous borders
- New patterns of economic growth and interaction
- A changing distribution of power, capabilities, and authority
- Increasing numbers of weak and disintegrating states
- Proliferation of various kinds of nonstate actors
- Emergence of new issues and alteration of traditional ones

While Rosenau does not believe these developments will result in an end to the state, he marshals weighty evidence showing that world affairs will no longer be dominated by state power. The broad scope of global politics, the arena within which political activities occur, and the relationships among actors are all changing drastically, says Rosenau, and will continue to do so.

---

ernability (Pittsburgh, PA: University of Pittsburgh Press, 2000); Roy Godson, ed., *Menace to Society: Political Criminal Collaboration Around the World* (New Brunswick, NJ: Transaction, 2003).

2. Rosenau, *Along the Domestic-Foreign Frontier: Exploring Governance in a Turbulent World* (Cambridge: Cambridge University Press, 2001).

Integration and Fragmentation

At the center of this new global milieu lie the interactive and seemingly contradictory processes of fragmentation and integration, which give rise to new spheres of power and authority. Fostering these interrelated phenomena are technological innovations in transportation and communications.

Integration, wrote Rosenau, is reflected in the internationalization of capital and growth of markets, the expansion of regional and transnational corporations and organizations, the spread of shared norms (democratic practices, human rights, environmental protection, free enterprise), and the interdependence of issues.[3]

Integration's antithesis, fragmentation, is the result of a continuing allegiance to traditional or particularistic values and practices (i.e., ethnicity, ethnonationalism, and religious fundamentalism), a weakening of state authority, and the growing influence of armed groups at both the substate and the transstate levels.

Because fragmentation and integration alter the structure of a global politics anchored in the nation-state, other diverse sources of power and authority—subsumed under the rubric of nonstate actors—now challenge the preeminence of the state. Bifurcation of world politics is the result. Moreover, a major outcome of bifurcation is growing violent discord between one category of increasingly powerful nonstate actors—armed groups—and increasingly weakened states.

---

3. It is possible for a state to be part of this integration, at least at the economic level, without adopting the shared norms identified by Rosenau. China is a case in point. In addition to Rosenau, see James E. Dougherty and Robert L. Pfaltzgraff Jr., *Contending Theories of International Relations,* 5th ed. (Reading, MA: Addison Wesley Longman, 2001); Michael Doyle and G. John Ikenberry, eds., *New Thinking in International Relations Theory* (Boulder, CO: Westview, 1997); and Barry Buzan and Richard Little, *International Systems in World History: Remaking the Study of International Relations* (New York: Oxford University Press, 2000).

Fragmentation and Failing States

Since 1945, the number of states has expanded from 51 to nearly 200. In almost every instance, these new governments, upon achieving independence, were granted sovereignty and the imprimatur of legitimacy from the United Nations. For many of them, however, achieving domestic legitimacy proved much more difficult. According to Robert Rotberg: "The decade plus since the end of the Cold War has witnessed a cascading plethora of [these] state failures, mostly in Africa but also in Asia. In addition, more and more states are at risk, exhibiting acute signs of weakness and/or the likelihood of outright failure."[4] Fragmentation escalated as armed groups increasingly challenged the authority and ability of states to rule, using a variety of means, including terrorism, guerrilla insurgency, and other irregular and unconventional forms of organized violence. Several internal wars resulted.

The primary cause of these internal wars today can be found in the state's "domestic politics." The critical factor determining whether a state is viable or failing, according to K. J. Holsti, is legitimacy.[5] Strong and healthy states exhibit several common characteristics or measures of legitimacy. First, there is an implicit social

4. Robert I. Rotberg, "Nation-State Failure: A Recurring Phenomenon?" This paper was prepared for the NIC's project on the shape of the world in 2015, available at www.cia.gov/nic/NIC_home.html. See also Rotberg, ed., *When States Fail: Causes and Consequences* (Princeton, NJ: Princeton University Press, 2004).

5. K. J. Holsti, *The State, War, and the State of War* (Cambridge: Cambridge University Press, 1996), 15; Donald M. Snow, *Distant Thunder: Patterns of Conflict in the Developing World,* 2nd ed. (New York: M. E. Sharpe, 1997); Snow, *Uncivil Wars: International Security and the New Internal Conflicts* (Boulder, CO: Lynne-Rienner, 1996); William E. Odom, *On Internal War: American and Soviet Approaches to Third World Clients and Insurgents* (Durham, NC: Duke University Press, 2003); *Small Wars and Insurgencies Journal Special Issue: Non-State Threats and Future Wars* 13, no. 2 (Autumn 2002); and Gurr, "Communal Conflicts and Global Security," *Current History* (May 1995).

contract between state and society, the latter comprising all ethnic, religious, political, and economic groupings. In other words, there is agreement on the political "rules of the game." Citizens feel loyalty to the state, the political principles upon which it is based, and its institutions. Second, while legitimacy allows the state to extract resources, it also requires that the state provide services and a reasonable amount of order, law, and security. Third, a clear boundary must exist between public service and personal gain. In other words, state power is not a platform for personal enrichment. Finally, no group is excluded from seeking political influence or receiving a fair share of resources and services because of its affiliation.

In the late twentieth century, government legitimacy was eroding in many Third World states and was failing to take root in a number of post-communist states, according to the Minorities at Risk Project.[6] Based on data from this study, Monty Marshall and Ted Robert Gurr found that when compared with the high-water mark of the mid-1990s, internal or societal armed conflict was somewhat reduced in 2002. That is the good news. They also explain, however, that these trends are fragile: "[P]ositive trends coexist with counter-trends that present major challenges to the emerging global community."[7] Among the countertrends are the enduring causes of failing and failed states—weakened capacity, deeply divided societies, devastated economies, squandered resources, traumatized populations, civil societies crippled by war, international organized crime, and black market networks.[8]

Chester Crocker summarized this situation succinctly: "Self-

6. The Minorities at Risk Project website, www.cidcm.umd.edu/inscr/mar/data.htm, allows easy access to this data set and also provides up-to-date qualitative assessments for each communal group.

7. Marshall and Gurr, *Peace and Conflict 2003* (College Park, MD: Center for International Development and Conflict Management, 2003), 1, 15.

8. Ibid.

interested rulers . . . progressively corrupt the central organs of government," and they "ally themselves with criminal networks to divide the spoils." The authority of the state is "undermined, . . . paving the way for illegal operations." In conjunction with these developments, "state security services lose their monopoly on the instruments of violence, leading to a downward spiral of lawlessness." Crocker concluded, "When state failure sets in, the balance of power shifts . . . in favor of armed entities [groups] outside the law" who "find space in the vacuums left by declining or transitional states."[9]

Lawless/Ungoverned Territory

In turn, the "vacuum left by declining or transitional states" results in the expansion of lawless and ungoverned areas. This creates safe havens in which armed groups can establish secure bases for self-protection, training, planning, and launching operations against local, regional, and global targets. Terrorist groups, as well as insurgent and criminal organizations, are located in the remote parts of more than twenty countries. These areas are distinguished by rugged terrain, poor accessibility, low population density, and little government presence.

For example, the confluence of such territory in several Central Asian states has made that region home to several armed groups: a nascent Afghani insurgency based in the tribal areas along the Pakistan border, Kashmiri insurgents located in Pakistan, the reduced insurgent movement in Uzbekistan, as well as elements of the Taliban and al Qaeda spread across this lawless area. Bin Laden himself is apparently hiding in the mountains of the North-West Frontier Province in Pakistan. In South America, about half of Colombia's national territory, abandoned for decades by the central

9. Crocker, "Engaging Failing States," *Foreign Affairs* (September/October 2003): 34–35.

government, is now controlled by a range of armed groups, including Marxist guerrillas, drug traffickers, and right-wing paramilitary groups, each pursuing its own political and social agenda and the defeat of the state.

Lawlessness and ungovernability are not confined to remote rural territories. They can also be found in cities located in failing states. As with more remote areas, urban areas can provide safe havens for armed groups. Mogadishu, in Somalia, is a case in point, as are the Pakistani cities of Karachi and Lahore. In the aftermath of the overthrow of the Taliban, many al Qaeda members redeployed to the safety of these cities, from which they can coordinate attacks, recruit members, and solicit funds to continue their holy war against America.

III. FRAMEWORK FOR CATEGORIZING AND DIFFERENTIATING ARMED GROUPS

Armed groups pose different analytical and operational challenges from those of states. However, like their state counterparts, armed groups are now able to acquire the capacity to execute violent strikes that can have a strategic impact on even the most powerful nation-state. This appears to be the case in terms of one type of armed group in particular—international terrorist organizations— as al Qaeda demonstrated on September 11. In addition to direct strategic threats, armed groups, such as international criminal organizations, can also challenge states in various indirect ways.

Indeed, during the past two decades, many states have been increasingly confronted by nonstate armed groups—militias, insurgents, terrorists, and criminal cartels—that operate both within and across state boundaries. With few exceptions, however, U.S. policy makers, and the security and intelligence organizations that serve them, failed to appreciate the growing salience of some nonstate armed groups and were loath to consider these groups tier-one security threats that could undermine major interests or carry out attacks that could have a strategic impact. Only states, it was thought, had such power.

An examination of the *National Security Strategy of the United States*, produced annually through the 1990s by the White House, bears this out.[10] While terrorist and criminal organizations were included, they were seen as secondary or tier-two or tier-three security problems, not requiring a military response. This point was driven home by the intelligence assessments of terrorist attacks against the United States, beginning with the first World Trade Center bombing in 1993. Indeed, throughout the 1990s, these terrorist strikes were classified as criminal acts, and few intelligence community officials and analysts were willing to consider these actions a clear and present danger to the United States—much less a form of war. Any attempt to describe terrorism in those terms ran into a stone wall of skepticism.[11]

A Taxonomy of Armed Groups[12]

What constitutes an armed group? How many are there? How should they be differentiated from one another and categorized? What motivates them? To what extent do they cooperate with one another, as well as with states and other nonstate actors? Can they be identified and countered in their emergent or incipient stage of development? Do armed groups provide policy opportunities, as well as threats, to policy? No taxonomy exists that rigorously

10. For the most current publication, see *National Security Strategy of the United States of America*, www.whitehouse.gov/nsc/nss.html.

11. This rejection of the belief that terrorism is a form of warfare was forcefully made by Paul Pillar, deputy chief of CIA's Counterterrorism Center, in his *Terrorism and U.S. Foreign Policy* (Washington, DC: Brookings, 2001).

12. This is drawn from Richard Shultz, Douglas Farah, Itamara V. Lochard, *Armed Groups: A Tier-One Security Priority* (Colorado Springs: U.S. Air Force Institute for National Security Studies, 2004), 14–30.

addresses these questions, even though armed groups are the subject of increasing attention worldwide.

Armed groups can be divided into four categories—insurgents, terrorists, militias, and organized crime. Consider first what they have in common.

First, all armed groups, to varying degrees, challenge the state's authority, power, and legitimacy. Some do so by seeking to overthrow the government and replace it, while others attempt to weaken, manipulate, or co-opt the state. Second, armed groups, at least in part, use violence and force, but in unconventional and asymmetric ways. It is true that some armed groups maintain political and paramilitary wings and that the former may, for tactical reasons, eschew violence. Still, the use of force is a critical instrument for these organizations, regardless of how they may seek to mask that fact. Violence is used instrumentally to achieve political and/or other objectives. Third, armed groups operate both locally and globally due to the developments of the information age, a point elaborated below. Thus, they are able to expand the battlefield to attack state adversaries both at home and abroad. Fourth, armed groups operate on a clandestine and conspiratorial basis. They are, in large part, secret organizations that seek to mask their infrastructure and operations. Fifth, all armed groups have factional and political rivalries. Finally, as noted above, armed groups are not democratically based organizations. They do not adhere to the rule of law to resolve disputes. Just the opposite is the case.

Insurgents, terrorists, militias, and criminal organizations also differ in critical ways. There is no generic or ideal type for any of these four variants. This is certainly true in terms of the basic characteristics of an armed group, which can be divided into the following six elements: (1) leadership, (2) rank-and-file membership, (3) organizational structure and functions, (4) ideology or political code of beliefs and objectives, (5) strategy and tactics, and (6) links with other nonstate and state actors. How armed groups approach these issues varies across and within the four categories, as the following taxonomy illustrates.

Insurgents

Insurgents can threaten the state with complex political and security challenges because of their organization and operation. One specialist defines insurgents as armed groups that "consciously use political resources and violence to destroy, reformulate, or sustain the basis of legitimacy of one or more aspects of politics."[13] While this description is a useful starting point, a more comprehensive delineation is necessary:

- *Insurgency* is a protracted political and military set of activities with the goal of partially or completely gaining control over the territory of a country. It involves the use of irregular military forces and illegal political organizations. The insurgents engage in actions ranging from guerrilla operations, terrorism, and sabotage to political mobilization, political action, intelligence and counterintelligence activities, and propaganda or psychological warfare. All of these instruments are designed to weaken or destroy the power and legitimacy of a ruling government, while at the same time increasing the power and legitimacy of the armed insurgent group.

Within the parameters of this definition, insurgent groups can and have taken a number of different organizational forms, ranging from complexly constructed political, intelligence, and military associations to narrowly structured conspiratorial groups.[14] The

13. Bard E. O'Neill, *Insurgency and Terrorism* (Washington, DC: Brassey's, 1990), 13.
14. Thomas H. Green, *Comparative Revolutionary Movements* (Englewood Cliffs, NJ: Prentice Hall, 1990); Jack A. Goldstone, Tedd Robert Gurr, and Farrokh Moshiri, eds., *Revolutions of the Late Twentieth Century* (Boulder, CO: Westview, 1991); Anthony James Joes, *Guerrilla Warfare: A Historical, Biographical, and*

former is designed to mobilize supporters and establish an alternative political authority to the existing government, while employing intelligence and military means to attack and weaken the state
through escalating violence—the classic insurgent model. The latter
focuses on using violence to undermine the will of a government to
sustain losses and stay in the fight—not on controlling a particular
territory and building a parallel political apparatus in it.

Also affecting the approach taken by insurgents is the area or
terrain in which they carry out their activities. Whether they act in
cities, in a rural environment, or transnationally will have an
impact on how they approach each of the characteristics or elements of an armed group—organization, ideology, motivation, leadership, and membership background.

Where armed insurgent groups operate, the objectives they pursue and the organizational approach they adopt will shape the
strategy employed. In the classic insurgent model, the strategy goes
through four stages—preinsurgency, organizational/infrastructure
development, guerrilla warfare, and mobile conventional warfare.
This process can extend over a very long time. However, not all
insurgencies seek to go through all four stages, and this will affect
how they employ unconventional paramilitary tactics, including
guerrilla warfare, terrorism, and sabotage. Often, insurgents
receive assistance from states and, increasingly today, from other
nonstate actors,[15] which also affects each group's organizational
and operational profile.

Finally, armed insurgent groups have pursued very different

Bibliographical Sourcebook (Westport, CT: Greenwood Press, 1996); Mustafa
Rejai, *The Comparative Study of Revolutionary Strategy* (New York: McKay,
1977); Walter Laqueur, *Guerrilla: A Historical and Cultural Study* (Boston: Little
Brown, 1976); James DeFronzo, *Revolutions and Revolutionary Movements*
(Boulder, CO: Westview, 1991); and Paul Berman, *Revolutionary Organizations*
(Lexington, MA: Lexington Books, 1974).

15. Daniel Byman, et al., *Trends in Outside Support for Insurgent Movements*
(Santa Monica, CA: RAND, 2001).

objectives. During the Cold War, left-wing revolutionary and national liberation movements employed insurgency strategies. These movements took considerable time to establish complex political structures as a prelude to carrying out military operations. Their overall objective was to overthrow the state and carry out radical political and social change.

In the 1980s, this objective began to change. New types of insurgent movements appeared, based on existing ethnic and religious identities, which had a profound impact on the objectives pursued. Examples of ethnically driven insurgents include the Democratic Party (DPK) and Patriotic Union (PUK) of Kurdistan, the Northern Alliance in Afghanistan, the armed clans fighting the Russians in Chechnya, and the Liberation Tigers of Tamil Eel (LTTE). Religious cases include the People's Liberation Army (SPLA) and People's Liberation Movement (SPLM) of Sudan, various Sikh and Kashmiri factions in India, and Hezbollah in Lebanon.

Are there incipient or nascent indicators that a state can identify before an insurgency rises to the level of a serious threat to the state's stability and security? Yes, and this is true not just for insurgents but also for each of the armed groups included in the taxonomy. However, most states faced with such challenges fail to see the early telltale signs and, consequently, do not take the necessary steps to prevent the situation from escalating. According to interviews with senior-level Pentagon and CIA officials, this is certainly true of the U.S. government. These officials doubted that such early and preventive steps are possible, given the existing organizational cultures in each agency.[16] Nevertheless, these indicators do exist, and they can be observed if the intelligence and security agencies are structured to do so.

For example, a new group seeking to mount an insurgency must

16. Confidential interviews with Department of Defense and CIA officials conducted in 2004.

take certain steps. First, it must build an organization. If the state is vigilant, it can see early signs, such as the departure of a number of individuals from their homes for training and indoctrination or the defection of a noticeable number of members from moderate political parties. Increasingly radical political proselytizing by members of previously unknown political groups would be another early indicator, as would the discovery of small but growing amounts of arms and other materials needed for an insurgency. Fund-raising efforts to purchase these necessities would constitute additional supporting evidence of the beginnings of an insurgency.

These and other early warning signs of the emergence of an insurgency do not take place in the dark. All are discernible. Intelligence and security services can discover them at the beginning or preinsurgency stage of development. But to do so, a new way of thinking has to be bred into the organizational culture of the intelligence and security services.

Terrorists

Terrorism, and the armed groups that employ it, has been defined in myriad ways.[17] Moreover, since the latter 1970s, "terrorism" has

---

17. See Russell Howard and Reid Sawyer, eds., *Terrorism and Counterterrorism: Understanding the New Security Environment* (Guilford, CT: McGraw Hill, 2004); Bruce Hoffman, *Inside Terrorism* (New York: Columbia University Press, 1998); Pillar, *Terrorism and U.S. Foreign Policy* (Washington, DC: Brookings, 2001); Eqbal Ahmad and David Barsamian, *Terrorism: Theirs and Ours* (New York: Seven Stories Press, 2001); Cindy Combs, *Terrorism in the Twenty-First Century* (Upper Saddle River, NJ: Prentice Hall, 1997); Thomas Badey, "Defining International Terrorism: A Pragmatic Approach," *Terrorism and Political Violence* (Spring 1998); C. J. M. Drake, "The Role of Ideology in Terrorists' Target Selection," *Terrorism and Political Violence* (Summer 1998); and Hoffman, "The Confluence of International and Domestic Trends in Terrorism," *Terrorism and Political Violence* (Summer 1997). In addition, there are academic journals devoted to the topic, including *Studies in Conflict and Terrorism* and *Terrorism and Political Violence*.

frequently been used as a rhetorical tool to discredit and delegiti-mize. With that in mind, a more operational definition is useful:

- *Terrorism* is the deliberate creation and exploitation of fear by an armed group through the threat and/or use of the most pro-scribed kind of violence for political purposes, whether in favor of or in opposition to an established government. The act is designed to have a far-reaching psychological effect beyond the immediate target of the attack and to instill fear in and intimi-date a wider audience. The targets of terrorist groups increas-ingly are noncombatants, and under international norms, large numbers of them have the status of protected individuals and groups.

Terrorists differ from insurgents in several ways, beginning with tactics and targeting. Insurgents use a number of political and paramilitary tactics, of which terrorism frequently has been only one. Terrorist groups, on the other hand, have a narrower opera-tional approach that increasingly focuses on targeting noncombat-ants. Through the 1990s, terrorist groups were progressively more indiscriminate in their targeting, seeking to kill as many noncom-batants as possible.

As with insurgents, terrorist groups in the 1990s were motivated less by left-wing ideologies and more by ethnicity and religion. According to the RAND–St. Andrews University index, approximately half of all known terrorist groups were religiously driven.[18] Furthermore, an overwhelming majority of these groups are located in the Islamic world. This is in contrast to the 1970s and 1980s, when terrorists tended to be organized into smaller groups and were inspired by left-wing ideologies.

Another important difference between terrorist and insurgent

18. The database can be found at the Centre for the Study of Terrorism and Political Violence, St. Andrew's University (UK), www.st-andrews.ac.uk/intrel/research/cstpv/.

armed groups is the extent to which the former establish links and cooperative arrangements. During the 1990s, al Qaeda created an elaborate set of connections with a significant number of like-minded terrorist groups in as many as sixty countries. In effect, al Qaeda established a multinational alliance of armed groups that can operate in their originating states as well as transnationally. It also developed a sophisticated financial network for collecting and transferring money for the organization and its operations.[19]

As with an insurgent movement, there are incipient indicators that a state can identify before a terrorist group rises to the level of a serious threat. Given that some terrorist groups can be quite small, however, detecting these indicators is difficult. Nevertheless, such groups still have to establish a clandestine organization, recruit and train personnel, acquire resources, meet and communicate, and so on. Although they do so in secret, it is possible to monitor these activities.

As more is learned about al Qaeda's origins, early stages, and maturation, it becomes apparent that early warning indicators were available for the U.S. intelligence community (IC) to collect and analyze. However, such an approach is usually not part of the IC culture.

Militias

With the growing number of weak and failing states in the 1990s, a third category of armed groups—militias—became more numerous and prominent.[20] Militias appear to thrive, in particular, in

---

19. Rohan Gunaratna, *Inside Al Qaeda: A Global Network of Terror* (New York: Columbia University Press, 2002), and Douglas Farah, *Blood from Stones: The Secret Financial Network of Terror* (New York: Broadway Books, 2004).

20. Ralph Peters, *Fighting for the Future: Will America Triumph?* (Harrisburg, PA: Stackpole Books, 1999); and Alice Hills, "Warlords, Militia, and Conflict in Contemporary Africa: A Re-examination of Terms," *Small Wars and Insurgencies* (Spring 1997).

states with ineffectual central governments and to benefit from a global black market. While individual militias received considerable international attention, particularly those in Africa and Central Asia, there have been few attempts to define this type of armed group in a systematic way or to identify different subtypes. Indeed, of the four variants in our taxonomy, the literature on militias is, from an analytic perspective, by far the weakest.

Based on post–Cold War examples, armed militia groups appear to share the following characteristics:

- A *militia*, in today's context, is a recognizable irregular armed force operating within the territory of a weak or failing state. The members of militias often come from the under classes and tend to be composed of young males who are drawn into this milieu because it gives them access to money, resources, power, and security. Not infrequently, members are forced to join; in other instances, membership is seen as an opportunity or a duty. Militias can represent specific ethnic, religious, tribal, clan, or other communal groups. They may operate under the auspices of a factional leader, clan, or ethnic group or on their own after the breakup of the state's forces. They may also be in the service of the state, either directly or indirectly. In general, members of militias receive no formal military training. Nevertheless, in some cases, they are skilled unconventional fighters. In other instances, they are nothing more than a gang of extremely violent thugs who prey on the civilian population.

Militias so defined can vary widely in terms of how they organize, recruit, operate, and conduct themselves. Of the four armed group variants in the taxonomy, militias are the most amorphous.

Several militias that emerged since the latter 1980s have been brutal in their use of violence, directing it more at civilians than at soldiers or other militias. In fact, in conflicts involving militias, civilians are frequently the target, as has been the case in Africa.

Untrained militia groups, often made up of youth who are forced to join and compelled to take part in initiation rituals involving frightful human rights abuses, have been guilty of unspeakable crimes and atrocities, even against the tribe or clan they claim to represent.

Consider the situation in Côte d'Ivoire in the 1990s. Both anti- and pro- government militias were charged with widespread maltreatment of civilians. According to Human Rights Watch, these militias carried out "systematic and indiscriminate attacks on civilians, [including] summary executions, arbitrary arrest and detention, disappearances, torture, rape, pillage, corporal punishment, and other violent acts."[21]

In other parts of the world, militias have been more disciplined, less abusive of the population in general and of their own ethnic tribe or clan in particular, and led by men interested in local or regional political power. Afghanistan is a case in point. Still, there is no generic Afghan militia. Rather, militias there include various formations comprising former mujahideen commanders, tribal contingents, seasonal conscripts, and foreign volunteers. The combat potential of these units varies considerably, ranging in strength from a few dozen to several hundred fighters, depending on the ability of their leaders and the resources available. To be sure, Afghan militias and their leaders threaten both the country's stability and the current attempt by the United States and the international community to build a post-Taliban government of unity.

Militias have been central players in the politics of other multiple-identity countries as well. This has been true in Lebanon, where many seem to be more loyal to their confessional group or clan than to their country. For example, in the latter 1970s, when Lebanon plunged into civil war, and through the early 1990s, confessional factions and their militias were locked in an intractable

---

21. Human Rights Watch, "Côte d'Ivoire: Militias Commit Abuses with Impunity," *Human Rights News* (November 27, 2003), www.hrw.org/press/2003/11/cote112703.htm.

political fight in which Sunnis fought Shiites, Maronites fought Druze, Christians fought Muslims, and so on. When the civil war ended in the early 1990s, demobilizing these militias was not easy. But eventually, it was accomplished, and the Lebanese Armed Forces (LAF) began to slowly rebuild itself as Lebanon's only major nonsectarian institution. The LAF has extended central government authority over about two-thirds of the country. However, Hezbollah retains its weapons and militia forces.

Another way militias differ among themselves has to do with leadership. There are those operating under the control of a recognized and powerful leader, like the late General Aideed in Somalia. Clan militias, however, function under decentralized collective leaderships that seek to protect or advance the interests of the clan; there is no one identifiable leader. Many of the armed groups in Chechnya fit this description.

Where strong militia leaders exist, "warlord" is often used in the media to describe them. As with other terminology employed to describe militias, this term also lacks analytic clarity. What is a warlord and how does he operate as a militia leader? One specialist describes modern-day warlords as "local strongmen able to control an area and exploit its resources and people while . . . keeping a weak authority at bay. Warlords' motives range from the advancement of clan, tribe, or ethnic goals to political ambition, localized power, and personal wealth."[22] Such individuals as General Rashid Dostum (Afghanistan), General Aideed (Somalia), Walid Jumblat (Lebanon), Charles Taylor (Liberia), and Colonel Khudoiberidyev (Tajikistan) are all prominent examples from the 1990s.[23] Even so, among these individuals, there are important differences that the generic label "warlord" obscures.

These examples illustrate how widely militias can differ. Any

22. Hills, "Warlords, Militias, and Conflict," 40.
23. Ibid., and John MacKinlay, "War Lords," *RUSI Journal* (April 1998).

attempt to categorize them by how they organize, recruit, operate, and behave requires close attention to the cultural and political context in which they exist.

Militias have had an impact beyond the borders of the states in which they operate, and in the aftermath of the Cold War, they have engaged U.S. interests and policy. As a result, Washington has had to come to appreciate the complex nature of these disparate armed groups. Doing so has proved thorny, and, not infrequently, the United States has found itself in situations where it has been bereft of such knowledge and suffered the consequences.

Consider the U.S. intervention in Afghanistan following September 11. To understand what goes on inside Afghan borders, the key unit of analysis remains the tribe, even in the twenty-first century. This was the reality Washington faced in fall 2001, when it went to war with the Taliban, a radical Islamist regime that for several years had given sanctuary and succor to al Qaeda.

Washington aligned with the Northern Alliance, a loose grouping of different tribal factions—Hazaras, Tajiks, Uzbeks—that had been fighting the Taliban for years. The Alliance reflected the traditional nature of politics and society in Afghanistan, where tribal groups and their leaders are central actors. The Department of Defense and the CIA were unable to incorporate the majority Pashtun tribe into their operations. Although at the time it proved unnecessary, this decision had long-term implications that a sophisticated understanding of Afghanistan's tribal system would have signaled. In the aftermath of the war, Washington found this expedient decision to ride the Northern Alliance to a quick victory to be costly. To stabilize and unify Afghanistan, Washington had to bring all of the tribes together, demobilize their militias, and establish a national government of unity. This turned out to be tricky given both the course of action Washington pursued in fall 2001 and its belated understanding of Afghanistan's complicated tribal system.

As with insurgent and terrorist groups, there are incipient indicators that can be identified before a militia group rises to the level of serious threats to both regional stability and U.S. interests. Information on the indicators I have highlighted can be collected and analyzed. However, to do so requires an intelligence service that not only is geared to spot such developments early on but also has a mature understanding of the culture and the traditional setting in which militia groups flourish.

Criminal Organizations

The final category of armed groups is that of criminal organizations. While certainly not new, this group has grown as a dangerous threat to individual states and the international system. The wealth and power of these organizations has burgeoned over the past twenty-five years, and several have established international links and networks.

Armed criminal groups today exhibit several characteristics. First, they possess an identifiable structure and leadership that have as their purpose operation outside the law in a particular criminal activity. They maintain hierarchical arrangements with clearly demarcated leadership-subordinate roles, through which the group's goals are advanced. As such armed groups mature, they no longer rely on the leadership of one or a few individuals for their survival.

Second, these armed groups can take different forms and "operate over time [and space] not just for ephemeral [or temporary] purposes."[24] That is to say, they engage in more than one type of

24. Godson and William J. Olson, *International Organized Crime: Emerging Threat to U.S. Security* (Washington, DC: National Strategy Information Center, 1993), 4. Also see Bailey and Godson, eds., *Organized Crime and Democratic Governability*; Godson, ed., *Menace to Society: Political Criminal Collaboration Around the World* (Piscataway, NJ: Transaction Publishers); Phil Williams, "Transnational Criminal Organizations: Strategic Alliances," *Washington Quarterly* (Winter 1995): 57–72; United Nations Office on Drugs and Crime, www

criminal enterprise and operate over large parts of a region or around the globe.

Third, armed criminal groups maintain internal cohesion and loyalty through ethnicity and the family ties of its members. They are anchored in a "community, family, or ethnic base." This provides the armed group with a code of behavior that entails "allegiance, rituals, [and] ethnic bonds . . . [to] help to engage the compliance and loyalty of individuals within the organization."[25] These "ties that bind" allow group members to trust one another in ways that are very personal, reducing the likelihood of law enforcement infiltrating the group.

Fourth, criminal organizations employ violence "to promote and protect their interests." The violence can be directed externally against rivals to intimidate them or eliminate them as competitors. Internally, the violence maintains discipline and loyalty. Although criminal organizations vary in the extent to which they employ violence, all do so "for business purposes."[26] If violence is the stick, then bribery is the carrot used by criminal organizations. The availability of cash, in large quantities, is used to corrupt police and other government officials.

Finally, each of these characteristics contributes to the penultimate feature that distinguishes criminal organizations from other armed groups—they seek to make as much money as possible from their illegal activities, much like a legitimate business. The quest for money, and the power that goes with it, drives and sustains armed criminal groups.

The following definition emerges:

.unodc.org/unodc/en/organized_crime.html; Nathanson Centre for the Study of Organized Crime and Corruption, www.yorku.ca/nathanson/Links/links.htm; Center for Strategic and International Studies Organized Crime Project, www.csis.org/tnt/; Jane's Intelligence Review, jir.janes.com/; The Narco News Bulletin, www.narconews.com.

25. Godson and Olson, *International Organized Crime*, 4, 6.

26. Ibid., 6.

- An *armed criminal group* possesses a clandestine hierarchical structure and leadership whose primary purpose is to operate outside the law in a particular criminal enterprise. Such groups frequently engage in more than one type of criminal activity and can operate over large areas of a region and globally. Often, these groups have a family or ethnic base that enhances the cohesion and security of its members. These armed groups typically maintain their position through the threat or use of violence, corruption of public officials, graft, or extortion. The widespread political, economic, social, and technological changes occurring within the world allow organized crime groups to pursue their penultimate objective—to make as much money as possible from illegal activities—in ways that their earlier counterparts could not.

Major international criminal organizations (ICOs) have established links with other armed groups, and not just criminal ones. One of the more significant developments since the end of the Cold War is the burgeoning involvement of insurgents, terrorists, and militia groups in criminal activities. Unable to rely on outside aid from state sponsors, which can be fleeting, many insurgent and terrorist groups diversify their resource base by becoming involved with international criminal organizations. For ICOs, these partnerships are equally valuable, widening the scope and profitability of their operations.

A case in point is Hezbollah. Although Iran has been its patron, providing significant assistance, Hezbollah has been involved in drug trafficking as another way of financing its activities. It provides opium production and transshipment protection to criminal organizations in exchange for financial and other kinds of support.[27] In

---

27. Magnus Ranstorp, *Hiz'ballah in Lebanon* (New York: St. Martin's Press, 1997).

Afghanistan, various armed ethnic groups are involved in similar activities, as was al Qaeda.[28]

Another example can be found in Colombia. Since the late 1980s, insurgents there have not been able to rely on financial support from states that once backed them. Therefore, some insurgent fronts of the Revolutionary Armed Forces of Colombia (FARC) and the National Liberation Army (ELN) generate substantial revenue by taxing and protecting criminal enterprises involved in coca cultivation, cocaine processing, and drug shipments in the areas they control. It is estimated that this provides FARC with as much as half of its revenues. For the criminal groups, this collaboration provides safe haven in which production can flourish. At the same time, official government support for paramilitary self-defense groups, which control up to one-third of the national territory, has waned. In recent years, groups such as United Self Defense of Colombia (AUC) have turned to drug trafficking for economic support, allying with leaders of Colombia's heroin trade as well as with the cocaine cartels.[29]

Another link that enhances the power of ICOs is the active partnership between political actors—officeholders and the staff of the legal-governmental establishment of a state—and criminal actors. These arrangements, termed the political criminal nexus (PCN), consist of varying degrees of cooperation among political and criminal participants at the local, national, and transnational levels.[30]

28. Gunaratna, *Inside Al Qaeda*.

29. Alberto Garrido, *Guerrilla y el Plan Colombia: Hablan las FARC y el ELN* (Caracas, Venezuela: Producciones Karol, 2001); Thomas Marks, *Colombian Army Adaptation to FARC Insurgency* (Carlisle Barracks, PA: Strategic Studies Institute, U.S. Army War College, 2002); Bailey and Godson, eds., *Organized Crime and Democratic Governability*; and Godson, ed., *Menace to Society*.

30. Godson, ed., *Menace to Society*.

Enhancing the Power of Armed Groups

The potential power of armed groups was enhanced in the 1990s by three factors: globalization, information-age technology, and network-based approaches to organization.[31] Each factor provided armed groups with the opportunity to operate in ways that their earlier counterparts could never have imagined. As illustrated below, this is especially true for international criminal and terrorist organizations. While these three factors have been touched on previously, they need to be highlighted here to show how each affords armed groups the potential capacity to attack even the most powerful states, either directly or indirectly.

Globalization erodes the traditional boundaries that separated and secured the nation-state.[32] It allows people, goods, information, ideas, values, and organizations to move across international space without heeding state borders. Anyone with the necessary resources can do so. Modern transportation and communications systems, the movement of capital, industrial and commercial trends, and the post–Cold War breakdown of political and economic barriers, not only in Europe but also around the world, accelerate the globalization process.

Information-age technologies are central to globalization. These are the networks through which communications take place—instantaneously—on a worldwide basis. Cellular and satellite phones allow contact between the most remote and the most accessible locations of the globe. Computers and the Internet are the other pillars of the information revolution. According to Kegley and

31. John Arquilla and David Ronfeldt, eds., *Networks and Netwars: The Future of Terror, Crime, and Militancy* (Santa Monica, CA: RAND, 2001).

32. Rosenau wrote, "[W]hat distinguishes globalizing processes is that they are not hindered or prevented by territorial or jurisdictional barriers. They can spread readily across national boundaries and are capable of reaching into any community anywhere in the world." Rosenau, *Along the Domestic-Foreign Frontier*, 80.

Wittkopf, "No area of the world and no area of politics, economics, society, or culture is immune from the pervasive influence of computer technology."[33]

To take advantage of globalization and information-age technologies, nonstate armed groups adopt new organizational strategies that are less hierarchical and more networked. They follow the lead of the business community, which is in the forefront of such change. Small and large corporations have developed virtual or networked organizations that are able to adapt to the information age and globalization.[34]

The organizational design is more flat than pyramidal, with less emphasis on control from a central headquarters. Decision making and operations are decentralized, permitting local autonomy, flexibility, and initiative. To operate globally, network-based organizations require a capacity for constant communications among dispersed units, a capability afforded to them by the World Wide Web and cellular networks.[35] Globalization, information-age technology, and network-based organization empower not only international business but also armed groups to expand their activities across the world.

Consider how terrorist organizations have adapted to and taken advantage of globalization, information-age technology, and network-based organization. Most notable in this respect is al Qaeda. In a 1997 interview, bin Laden described his organization as "a product of globalization and a response to it."[36] To be sure, al

33. Kegley and Wittkopf, 272; Kakar, *Colors of Violence*; and Kaldor, *New and Old Wars*.

34. Charles Heckscher and Anne Donnelon, eds., *The Post-Bureaucratic Organization* (Thousand Oaks, CA: Sage, 1995).

35. Peter F. Drucker, "The Coming of the New Organization," *Harvard Business Review on Knowledge Management* (Boston, MA: Harvard Business Review Press, 1998), 3.

36. Foreign Policy Association, "In Focus—Al Qaeda," www.fpa.org/newsletter_info2478/newsletter_info.htm. See also Peter L. Bergen, *Holy War,*

Qaeda could not have operated in the 1980s as it did in the 1990s. As it did with international businesses, globalization had a huge impact on how and where al Qaeda organized and operated.[37]

Unlike hierarchically structured terrorist groups of the 1980s, the networked organization of dispersed units that bin Laden established prior to 9/11 were able to deploy nimbly, almost anywhere in the world. Al Qaeda's doctrine, configuration, strategy, and technology are all in harmonization with the information age. During the 1990s, it created an elaborate set of connections with fronts, several like-minded terrorist groups, other types of armed groups, and terrorist-sponsoring states. Information-age technologies and cyber networks allowed al Qaeda to recruit, communicate, establish cells, and attack targets globally. The pattern that emerged was a web of cells and affiliates around the world that could provide the intelligence and personnel needed to execute terrorist attacks against the United States and other targets. The 1998 East Africa Embassy bombings and the 9/11 attacks illustrate the phenomenon.[38]

Direct and Indirect Impact of Armed Groups

The developments outlined above make it possible for certain armed groups to attack asymmetrically and to strike at high-value or strategic targets of even the most powerful states. These attacks can have strategic consequences for the states' policies. This is a new phenomenon that requires states to change their behavior. Of course, not all armed groups that exist today can reach the level of power to constitute a tier-one threat to the United States.

Inc.: Inside the Secret World of Osama Bin Laden (New York: The Free Press, 2001), 222.

37. Gunaratna, *Inside Al Qaeda*.

38. Richard H. Shultz Jr. and Andreas Vogt, "The Real Intelligence Failure of 9/11 and the Case for a Doctrine of Striking First," in Howard and Sawyer, eds., *Terrorism and Counterterrorism: Understanding the New Security Environment.*

An asymmetrical attack is one that seeks to circumvent or undermine an adversary's strengths and exploit his weaknesses using methods that differ significantly from the adversary's mode of operation. While asymmetric options are a normal part of all wars, armed groups must pay closer attention to this approach because of the power differences between themselves and the states they are confronting. Given this imbalance, the asymmetrical techniques that armed groups employ fall into the irregular, unconventional, and paramilitary categories of armed violence and warfare.

States confronted by armed groups often do not understand the significance of those challenges and frequently downplay the dangers they produce. According to Colin Gray, asymmetric threats work, in part, by defeating a state's imagination. Gray argued that in the 1990s, the United States was "trapped in a time warp of obsolescent political, ethical, and strategic assumptions and practices."[39] Evidence of this proposition can be seen in how the U.S. intelligence community downplayed asymmetrical terrorist threats and even successful operations.[40] This lack of imagination coincided with the attainment by at least one armed group—al Qaeda—of the capacity to initiate operations against high-value U.S. targets—political, economic, and military—across the globe.

An armed group could achieve the same direct strategic impact on U.S. interests and policies using more standard forms of terrorist and insurgent violence. The insurgents, militias, and terrorists

39. Gray, *Modern Strategy* (New York: Oxford University Press, 1999); Gray, *A Second Nuclear Age* (Boulder, CO: Lynne-Reinner, 1999); Gray, *Strategy for Chaos: Revolutions in Military Affairs and the Evidence of History* (London and Portland, OR: Frank Cass, 2002); and Gray, "Handfuls of Heroes on Desperate Ventures: When Do Special Operations Succeed?" *Parameters* XXIX, no. 1 (Spring 1999).

40. *Joint Inquiry into Intelligence Community Activities Before and After the Terrorist Attacks of September 11, 2001* (December 2002), www.gpoaccess .gov/serialset/creports/911.html; Gunaratna, *Inside Al Qaeda*; and Shultz and Vogt, "The Real Intelligence Failure."

attacking coalition forces in Iraq are a case in point—their assaults have seriously and rapidly spiraled since the end of the conventional war in April 2003. This could have dire strategic consequences for U.S. foreign policy if it weakens Washington's commitment to its long-term reconstruction and democratization program for Iraq.

In addition to asymmetrical attacks against high-value targets, there are other indirect ways armed groups can affect the interests and policies of the United States. For example, they can destabilize states or regions that are of critical importance to the United States. These indirect threats, while not of the same magnitude as those described above, can nevertheless affect important U.S. interests in various ways. Take the example of regions where the stability and development of states is undermined by collaboration between the political establishment and armed criminal groups. In most instances, if a criminal group has endured and prospered, it has reached some type of accommodation with political authorities.[41]

Such active partnerships can undermine the rule of law, human rights, and economic development. They can also create ungoverned areas where armed groups can flourish. In some areas, such as Mexico, Nigeria, and Turkey, the problem of the PCN is chronic. In other countries and regions—Colombia, Afghanistan, the Balkans, and the Caucuses—the problem is more acute and violent and often can dominate political, economic, and social life.

These situations constitute security problems because they can interfere dramatically with the functioning of state and society, undermining political, economic, and social infrastructure. The instability generated can affect not only the state and region in which it takes place, but also U.S. policy interests. In each of the countries and regions with acute PCN problems discussed above, the U.S. interests range from important to vital.

41. Godson, ed., *Menace to Society*.

IV. U.S. INTELLIGENCE CULTURE: NOT PREPARED FOR
ARMED GROUP THREATS AND OPPORTUNITIES

During the Cold War and now in its aftermath, the U.S. intelligence community, and most importantly the CIA, has dealt with armed groups in an *episodic, transitory,* and *ad hoc* manner. This approach took root in the 1950s. However, even in those early days of the Cold War, insurgent and resistance groups began to appear and affected regional and international security. While they received some CIA attention, it was on a makeshift basis. This impromptu approach characterized the 1950s through the end of the 1970s, with one major exception.

The exception to this pattern occurred in the early 1960s. It came about at the strong behest of policy makers—in this case, the president. The Kennedy administration ushered in a period of heightened interest in both the threats and opportunities presented by armed groups. This entailed two missions—assisting and countering armed insurgent groups—that, at the time, were subsumed under the rubric of special warfare.

As a result, the intelligence community—the CIA in particular—expanded capabilities to respond to armed group challenges. According to one former senior officer who specialized in paramilitary operations (PM) at that time, the CIA established within its operational training program insurgency and counterinsurgency courses.[42] This had been mandated by the White House under National Security Action Memorandum 124, which directed that all agencies of the U.S. government with a role in special warfare must develop an infrastructure to support this new mission area. All those involved were to receive training, from the junior to the senior levels.[43]

42. Douglas Blaufarb, *The Counterinsurgency Era* (New York: Free Press, 1977), 66–74.
43. Ibid., 70.

While the extent to which this took place and the degree to which it was institutionalized within the CIA is not clear, in the field, particularly in Southeast Asia, the CIA established major operational programs both to counter communist insurgents and to assist anti-communist resistance. The common theme running through those efforts was training and mobilization of local forces, be they tribal, religious, or political.

Again, according to one former senior officer, "[V]ery little theorizing accompanied this process." In other words, no systematic doctrine was developed. Rather, operational programs grew out of "the intelligence agency's professional familiarity with the Communist styles and particularly its conclusion that the decisive answer to peoples' war was a similar strategy on the government's side. Support was therefore provided to host government efforts toward this goal." In addition, "the CIA sought and found opportunities to mobilize, train, and arm minorities with a natural antipathy toward communists."[44]

On the analytic side, at that time, analysts and their managers paid a great deal of attention to insurgency. They were encouraged to take in-house courses on the subject, as well as classes offered by other U.S. government agencies. A former analyst from that period said that writing on insurgency and counterinsurgency issues would get the analyst instant attention. Therefore, many focused on armed groups and movements.

However, it does not appear that a separate branch was set up for this purpose. Rather, the topic was covered within the geographical units of the Directorate of Intelligence (DI). The Southeast Asia branch is illustrative: The CIA developed an expertise in understanding how the insurgents operated within South Vietnam. This can be seen in the debate that took place within the U.S. intelligence community over how to understand and estimate the size

44. Ibid., 83.

and capabilities of the Viet Cong. By approaching the topic of armed insurgent groups through its geographical units, the DI avoided institutionalizing the analysis of such nonstate armed groups.

When the Vietnam War ended, so did the intelligence community's interest in insurgency and counterinsurgency. No doctrine or lessons learned were deduced. Policy changed and attention to armed groups at the CIA quickly evaporated. The Directorate of Operations (DO) returned to its state-centric focus on the Soviet Union and its clients. The considerable paramilitary capabilities built up during the 1960s were drastically downsized, as the numbers bear out.[45] By the end of the 1970s, there were few PM specialists left in the CIA. The withdrawal from Vietnam likewise brought an end to the attention given to insurgency in the DI. As a result of this drawdown, when the Reagan administration elevated the threats posed by armed groups to a tier-one national security priority, it found the intelligence community did not have the capabilities to respond to these challenges. The systems for dealing with insurgents, resistance movements, and terrorism had to be reconstituted almost from scratch.

Over the next several years after the drawdown, the experiences of the Kennedy administration were repeated. Again, at the strong behest of policy makers, the CIA expanded capabilities to meet armed-group challenges. For example, when in 1982, the CIA's Directorate of Intelligence established a new branch to address the issue of insurgency, it came about not because the leadership of the DI recognized the importance of insurgency as a security issue in need of analytic attention. Rather, the director of Central Intelligence, William Casey, tasked them to do so.

45. In the fist year of his stewardship, DCI Turner ordered the elimination of 820 positions in the Directorate of Operations. This substantial reduction was only the harbinger of a major exodus of analysts. According to one of the most distinguished among them, Ted Shackley, during the latter 1970s, "approximately 2,800 American career intelligence officers like myself retired, many prematurely." Theodore Shackley, *The Third Option* (New York: McGraw Hill, 1981), ix.

Also during the 1980s, units were established at the CIA to focus on other types of armed groups. In 1986, again at the initiative of DCI Casey, a Counterterrorist Center (CTC) was created and directed to preempt and disrupt terrorists. Made up of officers from the DI and DO, as well as from other parts of the intelligence community, CTC was to produce assessments of international terrorist groups and to implement counterterrorist operations to collect intelligence on and minimize the effectiveness of those groups.

While the CTC was potentially a significant development in recognizing the importance of the terrorist threat, the 9/11 Commission revealed that CTC has had a checkered history in the CIA and was generally considered an anachronism within its organizational culture. DCI Casey envisioned an offensively oriented outfit that would track down and attack terrorists globally.[46] This stirred up sharp opposition in the DO, where it was worried that CTC would divert resources and talent and get the CIA involved in risky operations that could have serious political consequences. There were also questions raised about characterizing terrorism as such a serious threat.

With the conclusion of the Casey era and the Iran-Contra scandal, CTC's initial mandate came to an abrupt end. It remained in existence but was bureaucratically marginalized. According to one recent account, "[T]he original 'war room' vision [of Casey's] for action teams and an offensive posture yielded to a more cautious, analytical, report-writing culture."[47] Within the U.S. government, terrorism came to be seen as a secondary security issue that should be treated as a judicial/criminal/law enforcement matter. The CIA had a role to play, but it was ancillary.

The Reagan administration tasked the paramilitary division of the DO to become involved in two major operations—Afghanistan

46. Duane Clarridge, *A Spy for All Seasons* (New York: Simon and Schuster, 1995).
47. Steve Call, *Ghost Wars* (New York: Penguin, 2004), 141.

and Nicaragua. The DO was ready for neither. As noted earlier, not only were paramilitary capabilities drastically reduced in the wake of Vietnam, but also there were no organizational lessons to draw upon. Moreover, the DO leadership saw these kinds of operations as having the potential to get the CIA in big trouble. Consequently, they resisted the Reagan administration's decision to resuscitate the paramilitary capability. Nevertheless, the CIA's paramilitary capabilities were built up for these missions.

With the end of the Reagan administration and then the end of the Cold War, the operational and analytic capabilities to deal with armed group challenges were drastically downsized. As in the Kennedy period, when policy changed, so did attention to armed groups.

During the post–Cold War 1990s, even as armed groups became a major security challenge for the United States, the intelligence community did not see them as such. Analytically, the only armed groups that received meaningful attention during the 1990s were terrorist organizations, mainly al Qaeda. The primary place for this analysis was within CTC. The various 9/11 reports reveal that some members of that unit understood the growing power and danger al Qaeda posed. But within the CIA, these CTC members were seen as going too far and were labeled the Manson Family.[48]

These reports paint an even more disturbing picture concerning the developing operational capabilities in the DO to fight terrorism. The trouble can be seen in the late 1990s, when the Clinton administration began to recognize the seriousness of the al Qaeda challenge and ordered the DO to conduct covert operations against it, including killing bin Laden and his chief lieutenants. But the DO did not have the capabilities to do so, as these studies spelled out. Furthermore, members of the Clandestine Service questioned whether the service should even be involved in such operations. According

48. Ibid., 454, 511, 518, 535.

to Staff Statement No. 7 of *The 9/11 Commission Report*, "[S]enior CIA officers told us they were morally and practically opposed to getting CIA into what might look like an assassination." In addition, "a former CTC chief said he would have refused an order to directly kill bin Laden."

How can we explain this pattern, which, as this brief review discloses, stretches over several decades and spans both the Cold War and the post–Cold War periods? *The 9/11 Commission Report* and other similar reports concluded that the answer lies in the structure of the intelligence community. The recommendations of the reports to fix the situation take the form of a plethora of management reforms that both the White House and Congress have embraced. Althoug important, these remedies are not sufficient. They overlook an important root cause of U.S. intelligence weakness. Missing in the reform movement is recognition that it is the intelligence community's culture—the way professionals think about and approach their jobs—not just its structure that accounts for the pattern highlighted above.

The intelligence community's conception of its mission, as well as its methods of collection, analysis, covert action, and counterintelligence, reflect deep Cold War roots that have been resistant to change. This is not surprising, given what we know about organizational culture and how it shapes the mind-set and intellectual constructs of senior officials and managers. Once a culture becomes established, it is passed on and engrained into each new generation of professionals early in their induction into the organization. The culture will influence how the organization defines challenges and opportunities. It determines how to organize, prioritize, and operate.

This enduring U.S. intelligence culture reflects these organizational dynamics. Thus, the intelligence community has been unable to provide the capabilities needed to deal with the phenomenon of armed groups and the major challenges they pose. In the aftermath of the Cold War, the dominant culture's standard operating principles remained intact. While traditional approaches may be effective against state threats like Iran, armed groups are not vulnerable to analytical and operational practices of an intelligence culture anchored in the previous century.

Thus, reformation of the intelligence community means, first, recognizing that armed groups pose major, even strategic, challenges. Then it means that policy makers must take the necessary steps to change the dominant intelligence culture to address those challenges. It is to this that we now turn.

V. IMPLICATIONS FOR U.S. INTELLIGENCE

Armed groups have changed the nature of conflict and war in today's international security environment. Developments in the 1990s enhanced the power and capabilities of armed groups to attack the United States and other states in ways that constitute direct and major security challenges. When these attacks rise to the level attained by al Qaeda or by the insurgents, terrorists, and militias fighting U.S. forces in Iraq, they should be considered as warfare and should be treated as such.

Armed groups will continue to pose serious and increasingly dangerous security challenges to states, including the United States, into the foreseeable future. There is little to suggest they are a temporary post–Cold War phenomenon. The following trends illustrate just the opposite:

1. The number of weak and failed states remains a significant and chronic problem. Where they exist, armed groups find a hospitable environment with relative freedom from government authority and control.

2. Topographical mapping of these lawless and ungoverned areas reveals that they cover a massive amount of territory, providing

armed groups with access to secure bases for training, planning, and launching operations locally, regionally, and globally.

3. Nonstate armed groups and internal/transnational conflicts represent the most recurrent cause of instability around the globe. And these groups are growing more lethal due to the acquisition and indiscriminate use of highly destructive weapons. Moreover, many of these conflicts, particularly those due to ethnic, religious, tribal, and communal differences, will remain vicious, long lasting, and difficult to terminate.

4. The gravity of this situation is further compounded by the publicly stated objective of several armed groups to acquire and use weapons of mass destruction.

These trends have important implications for American intelligence. There are several steps the United States should consider for dealing with a twenty-first century international security landscape in which armed groups—insurgents, terrorists, militias, and criminal organizations—will present a plethora of direct and indirect challenges.

Senior policy makers and intelligence community managers need to recognize that in the years ahead, armed groups will seek to attack the United States asymmetrically to strike at high-value targets. These attacks can have strategic consequences similar to and even greater than 9/11. While not all armed groups can reach a level similar to that of al Qaeda, it is probable that some will see al Qaeda's conduct of warfare as a model to emulate.

Policy makers and intelligence community managers also have to comprehend the complex nature of the armed group threat and its tier-one security status. In the 1990s, as armed groups proliferated in both number and power, Washington was inattentive and subsequently paid a steep price. Given the keen interest of some armed groups in acquiring and using WMD, policy makers and intelligence community managers can afford no such indifference in the years ahead.

The escalating role of armed groups in the international security environment of the twenty-first century should not be seen as only constituting threats to U.S. interests and security. In certain cases, armed groups may also provide opportunities that, if taken advantage of, could contribute to the attainment of U.S. foreign policy and national security objectives.

This evolving security setting will necessitate major changes in the U.S. intelligence community. Through the 1980s and 1990s, this community assessed armed groups as secondary and peripheral security issues and was unwilling to recognize their growing salience, linkages, and power. Even today, doubts may still remain in these agencies about whether any armed group can undermine major U.S. interests or carry out attacks that could have a strategic impact. That such attacks constitute a form of warfare likewise remains, in the intelligence community, a suspect proposition.

Consequently, the organizational culture of the intelligence agencies tasked with the analytical and operational responsibilities of dealing with armed groups requires major revision. That organizational culture is not geared to deal with the emerging strategic challenges of armed groups. Thus, a new organizational culture must be established that approaches armed groups as a tier-one priority.

Armed groups present complex analytic puzzles. Understanding them requires sophisticated tools for differentiating among them, as well as for constructing systematic profiles of how they organize and function. These analytical tools should serve as the basis for all source collection that will provide the information needed to build such profiles.

These profiles, in turn, should serve as the basis for developing intelligence and special operations options—political, informational, psychological, economic, and paramilitary—for responding to and degrading or destroying those armed groups that threaten the United States. They could also be employed to identify options for assisting those armed groups that provide the United States with potential opportunities.

These profiles should also be adapted not only for use against armed groups already directly or indirectly attacking the United States, but also for identifying armed groups in their nascent stages. This will allow the United States to take preventive measures, defusing a threat before an armed group reaches the stage of serious violence.

The profiles can likewise be employed to identify ways in which the United States may want to assist certain armed groups whose success will be advantageous to U.S. foreign policy objectives.

Finally, beyond major revisions in the culture of the intelligence agencies, the developments outlined here have other important implications for those agencies, including the need for each to establish new practical requirements to create the requisite intelligence doctrine, organization, training, and personnel to meet the armed groups challenge in the twenty-first century.

<table>
<tr><td>**2**</td></tr>
</table>

Truth to Power? Rethinking Intelligence Analysis

Gary J. Schmitt

THE 9/11 COMMISSION'S final report has surprising little to say about the craft of intelligence analysis. Out of nearly five hundred pages, probably no more than a half dozen are directly concerned with analysis. Given the major overhauls in the intelligence community proposed by the Commission and then enacted into law, the absence of an extended discussion about analysis is striking. It is all the more conspicuous because so much of the literature on surprise attacks (and on surprises more generally) focuses on the analytic failures leading up to the events in question. Why weren't "the dots" connected? How was the enemy able to deceive and mislead its opponent? What was the character of the particular myopia or methodological flaws that kept people in the dark until too late?

The Commission's report does not provide answers to these questions.

Nevertheless, the Commission does make one very large point about intelligence analysis that is important to note—and to examine. According to the Commission, the core analytic failure was one of a lack of "imagination."[1] As commissioner and former secretary of the Navy John Lehman remarked: When the Commission studied the government's "documents, the internal papers, the recommendations of the top advisers to presidents, we were shocked at the failure to grasp the extent of [the] evil that was stalking us."[2] Put simply, the government had not come to grips with the novelty and the gravity of the threat posed by Osama bin Laden. And it was the intelligence community's analysts—distracted by, and pulled in the direction of providing current intelligence for, an ever-expanding array of priorities—who failed to undertake the kind of strategic big-think assessment of al Qaeda that might have shaken the government from its bureaucratic and political lethargy.[3]

According to the Commission, prior to 9/11, the U.S. intelligence community had not issued a new national intelligence estimate (NIE)—the most prestigious and most authoritative analytic product of the whole intelligence community—on terrorism since 1995. And though the 1995 NIE had predicted future terrorist attacks against the United States, including in the United States, other than a perfunctory 1997 "update," the intelligence community did not produce any authoritative accounts of bin Laden, his organization, or the threat he posed to the country. In some measure, the Commission argued this was part and parcel of "the conventional wisdom before 9/11" with respect to the threat posed by bin Laden: He was undoubtedly dangerous, but he was nothing "radically new, posing a threat beyond any yet experienced." For those inside government who thought differently, they needed some way

1. See *The 9/11 Commission Report: Final Report of the National Commission on Terrorist Attacks upon the United States* (New York: W. W. Norton, 2004), 339–44.

2. Lehman, "America After 9/11." Remarks given at the Foreign Policy Research Institute Annual Dinner, November 9, 2004, www.fpri.org/fpriwire/1203.200412.lehman.americaafter911.html.

3. See *The 9/11 Commission Report*, 90–91.

to "at least spotlight the areas of dispute" and, potentially, generate new policies. In the past, according to the report, an NIE "has often played this role, and is sometimes controversial for this very reason." Indeed, "such assessments, which provoke widespread thought and debate, have a major impact on their recipients, often in a wider circle of decisionmakers." Yet, as already noted, there were no new NIEs, and, hence, by the Commission's lights, the intelligence community missed a critical opportunity to challenge the prevailing perception of the security problem posed by bin Laden and al Qaeda.[4]

The opportunity was missed, the report suggests, because with the end of the Cold War, the lack of clarity about who America's real long-term enemies were, and what our long-term policy goals would be, undermined the intelligence community's ability to plow resources into "long-term accumulation of intellectual capital" on any given topic. Whatever else the Cold War had brought, it "had at least one positive effect: [I]t created an environment in which managers and analysts could safely invest time and resources in basic research, detailed and reflective." Within the analytic community, "a university culture with its version of books and articles was giving way to the culture of the newsroom."[5]

Complaints about this trend in intelligence analysis are long standing, as is the implicit suggestion that the gold standard when it comes to analysis is the dispassionate approach of the university scholar.[6] What the government needs, in this view, is less its own

4. Ibid., 343.
5. Ibid., 90–91.
6. From the "Church Committee" (1975–1976) investigation of the U.S. intelligence community:

> The task of producing current intelligence—analyzing day-to-day events for quick dissemination—today occupies much of the resources of the DI [Directorate of Intelligence]. Responding to the growing demands for information of current concerns by policy makers for more coverage of more topics [sic], the DI has of necessity

in-house CNN than, in the words of one former House intelligence committee chair, an analytic arm that is the equivalent of "a world-class 'think tank.'"[7]

Of course, the notion that intelligence analysis, at its best, is removed from the day-to-day work of government, that it requires distance from policy making and policy makers, has deep roots in the American intelligence tradition. In perhaps the most influential book ever written on intelligence analysis—*Strategic Intelligence for American World Policy* (1949)—Sherman Kent spelled out a very specific approach to guide analytic practice in the post–World War II intelligence community. Kent, a Yale historian, former mem-

---

resorted to a "current events" approach to much of its research. There is less interest in and fewer resources have been devoted to in-depth analysis of problems with long-range importance to policy makers. . . . The "current events" approach has fostered the problem of "incremental analysis," the tendency to focus myopically on the latest piece of information without systematic consideration of an accumulated body of integrated evidence. Analysts in their haste to compile the day's traffic, tend to lose sight of underlying factors and relationships." (U.S. Senate, Select Committee to Study Governmental Operations with Respect to Intelligence Activities, *Final Report*, book 1: *Foreign and Military Intelligence*, 94th Cong., 2d sess., 1976, S. Rep. 94-755, 272–273).

And, more recently, as *The 9/11 Commission Report* noted, the

weakness in all-source and strategic analysis were [sic] highlighted by a panel, chaired by Admiral David Jeremiah, that critiqued the intelligence community's failure to foresee the nuclear weapons tests by India and Pakistan in 1998, as well as by the 1999 panel, chaired by Donald Rumsfeld, that discussed the community's limited ability to assess the ballistic missile threat to the United States (91).

7. Following the end of the Cold War, the House and Senate Intelligence Committees proposed legislation to reorganize American intelligence. One major element of their proposal was to create a centralized analytic center, divorced from any operational intelligence entities or policy departments; the intent was to create something of an academic setting for analysts. According to then House committee chairman Representative Dave McCurdy, the goal was to "create in one place, a world class 'think tank'" ("Intelligence Committee Chairmen Introduce Sweeping Reorganization Plan," Press Release, U.S. Senate Select Committee on Intelligence, February 5, 1992).

ber of the Office of Strategic Services (OSS), and, later, the de facto "founding father" of the NIE process as director of the Office of National Estimates, argued that the key to avoiding future surprises along the lines of Pearl Harbor was for analysts to become modern social scientists:

> Research is the only process which we of the liberal tradition are willing to admit is capable of giving us the truth, or a closer approximation to truth, than we now enjoy. . . . We insist, and have insisted for generations, that truth is to be approached, if not attained, through research guided by a systematic method. In the social sciences which very largely constitute the subject matter of strategic intelligence, there is such a method. It is much like the method of physical sciences.[8]

The great promise of the positivist approach to political and social matters was to predict future human behavior, be it of individual leaders or whole countries. Indeed, so great was this promise that Kent argued it might be possible to predict the likely action of a state even when that state had not yet made up its mind on a specific course of action. One didn't need access to a file drawer of secrets; to the contrary, such access might even be misleading. In 1950, for example, Stalin's spies could have searched high and low

---

8. Sherman Kent, *Strategic Intelligence for American World Policy* (Princeton, NJ: Princeton University Press, 1949; reprint with new preface, 1966), 155. To this day, Kent's book is the most widely read text on intelligence analysis ever written. Following the surprise invasion of South Korea by North Korea in 1950, Kent was asked to come back to Washington to help organize the Office of National Estimates (ONE), the new analytic unit tasked with producing comprehensive, forward-looking assessments. Kent was soon put in charge of ONE and held that post for more than fifteen years. Not surprisingly, as two long-time observers of American intelligence noted: "ONE and the process of developing NIEs bore a strong resemblance to the principles for analysis Kent described in *Strategic Intelligence*" (Bruce Berkowitz and Allan Goodman, *Strategic Intelligence for American National Security* [Princeton, NJ: Princeton University Press, 1989], 5). Even today, decades later, Kent's shadow hangs over the Directorate of Intelligence, with the DI's school for basic and specialized analytic training named "The Sherman Kent School for Intelligence Analysis."

inside the U.S. government for a document pertaining to the defense of South Korea by American forces if North Korea attacked—and they would have found nothing. The Truman administration had made no decision about defending South Korea and, to the extent it had thought about it at all, had downplayed Korea's strategic relevance. Hence, as Kent pointed out, "[I]f knowledge of the other man's intentions is to be divined through the reading of his intimate papers and one's own policy is to be set on the basis of what one discovers, here is a case where policy was on the rocks almost by definition."[9]

This approach to intelligence analysis was to be reinforced by the institutional arrangements for carrying it out. Even before the CIA was up and running, analysts in the research and analysis branch of the OSS were employing "the invisible mantle of social science objectivity" to argue for a unique position within the national security system. By their lights, "the antinomies of fact and value, scholarship and partisanship with which Max Weber had struggled so heroically had been largely resolved" and necessitated a break from the traditional intelligence–policy maker nexus.[10] In the past, both in the United States and elsewhere, intelligence analysis had been located in government agencies or departments directly involved in policy making and execution. Under the new paradigm, scholarly objectivity required separation from value-laden or interest-driven decision makers.[11] Creating a central

9. Kent, "Preface to the 1966 Edition," *Strategic Intelligence*, xxiv.
10. Barry M. Katz, *Foreign Intelligence: Research and Analysis in the Office of Strategic Services, 1942–1945* (Cambridge, MA: Harvard University Press, 1989), 14–15.
11. In 1968, Kent published a then-classified essay "Estimates and Influence" in *Studies in Intelligence*, an in-house CIA journal. Kent opens the essay with the following warning to intelligence analysts about the potential irrationalities and biases of the policy maker as a consumer of the intelligence product:

> There are a number of things about policymaking which the professional intelligence officer will not want to hear. For example, not all policy makers can be guaranteed to be free of policy predilections prior

repository for intelligence information followed from the problems identified in having separate intelligence bureaus prior to Pearl Harbor. But creating a centralized *and* independent agency was justified on broader ground. Accordingly, no policy making department should control the CIA, and, appropriately enough, its headquarters would be located in suburban Virginia—some distance from the Pentagon, the State Department, and even the White House.

Independence from policy making or budgetary preferences, of course, does not guarantee objectivity. For much of the Cold War, for example, the CIA had an institutional interest in acting as "the corrective" to Pentagon and military service estimates regarding Soviet military matters. Putting aside whether the CIA's own judgments were any more correct, the CIA definitely saw its prestige within the national security system as very much tied to this role. Moreover, over time, intelligence analysts, whether independent of

---

to the time they begin to be exposed to the product of the intelligence calling. Indeed, there will be some policy makers who could not pass a rudimentary test on the "facts of the matter" but who have the strongest views on what the policy should be and how to put it into effect. We do not need to inquire as to how these men got that way or why they stay that way, we need only realize that this kind of person is a fact of life.

Nor should we be surprised to realize that in any policy decision there are a number of issues which we who devote ourselves solely to foreign positive intelligence may almost by definition be innocent of. The bulk of them are, of course, purely domestic ones. . . . Our wish is, of course, to have our knowledge and wisdom about the foreign trouble spot show itself so deep and so complete that it will perforce determine the decision. The nature of our calling requires that we pretend as hard as we are able that the wish is indeed the fact and that the policy maker will invariably defer to our findings as opposed to the cries of some domestic lobby.

The essay is now available in a collection of essays (*Sherman Kent and the Board of National Estimates: Collected Essays*) published by the CIA's Center for the Study of Intelligence. It can be found at www.odci.gov/csi/books/shermankent/toc.html.

a department or not, will develop a set of views about particular issues, publish those assessments, defend them, and, in turn, have a vested interest in seeing those judgments upheld.[12] Finally, independence cannot really guarantee that analytic books are not being cooked because, ultimately, even the CIA must admit that it works at least for, and is subordinate to, the president. Rather, the underlying problem is that, with rare exceptions, most national estimates cannot help but be, in crucial respects, speculative in nature. "Hard facts" are few and far between and, more often than not, still need to be given a context by analysts for their meaning to become clear. As a former senior intelligence analyst admits:

> As intelligence grows broader, more strategic in nature, its susceptibility to interpretation . . . grows. . . . [I]n the end, judgment is required to attempt answers . . . [and] draw upon an individual's general sense of "the way the world works" . . . a coherent view of international politics. . . . This kind of understanding is inherently ideological . . . because it imposes an order . . . on a highly diffuse body of data and events. . . . Nothing else can overcome the modern curse of information glut. . . . Yet to lack this construct is to bring an immense shallowness of understanding to human affairs.[13]

12. An example of this phenomenon occurred early in the Reagan administration on the question of whether Moscow was supporting international terrorism. During the 1970s, CIA analysts had taken the view that Soviet support was minimal or nonexistent. As former director of Central Intelligence Robert Gates reported, "When Secretary of State Alexander Haig asserted that the Soviets were behind international terrorism, intelligence analysts initially set out, not to address the issue in all its aspects, but rather to prove the secretary wrong—to prove simply that the Soviets did not orchestrate all international terrorism. But in so doing they went too far themselves and failed in early drafts to describe extensive and well-documented indirect Soviet support for terrorist groups and their sponsors" (Robert M. Gates, "The CIA and Foreign Policy," *Foreign Affairs* [Winter 1987–88]: 221).

13. Graham Fuller, "Intelligence, Immaculately Conceived," *National Interest* (Winter 1991–92): 96–97. Fuller is a former national intelligence officer for the Near East and former vice chair of the National Intelligence Council.

But given this description of the analytic process, why is it that when an analytic finding by the intelligence community that calls into question a policy decision by an administration is leaked and reported by the media, virtually everyone in Washington still acts as though the president and his advisors have turned their back on the analyst's sound, unbiased opinion? Of course, the analyst's opinion may well be sound and the president's decision not. With rare exception, however, the opinion will be precisely that, an opinion—not indisputable fact.

Nor, more important, has the institutional independence mandated by Kent's social science positivism paid off with its promise of being able to make contingent predictions with any confidence. The literature on intelligence failures vastly outstrips case studies of successes.[14] Time and again, American intelligence has been surprised—and with them, American policy makers. From North Korea's invasion of South Korea in 1950 to Saddam's overrunning of Kuwait in 1990, more often than not, U.S. intelligence has missed the mark when it comes to predicting major events. It didn't see the Sino-Soviet split coming; it didn't understand the nature of Castro's Cuban revolution until it was too late; it rejected the idea that the Soviets would put nuclear-tipped missiles in Cuba; it was surprised by the Tet Offensive in Vietnam; it didn't see the Soviet military intervention in Afghanistan coming; and, until it was virtually a done deal, it failed to call the collapse of the Soviet Union. Indeed, so prevalent is "surprise"—both here and with other intelligence services around the world—that the scholarly norm is captured by Richard K. Bett's classic article on the topic, "Why Intelligence Failures Are Inevitable."[15]

14. For a brief overview of the issue, see Abram N. Shulsky and Gary J. Schmitt, *Silent Warfare: Understanding the World of Intelligence*, 3rd ed. (Washington, DC: Brassey's, 2002), 62–69.

15. Betts, "Analysis, War and Decision: Why Intelligence Failures Are Inevitable," *World Politics* (October 1978): 61–89. See also Ernest R. May, ed., *Know-*

Despite this record, the notion that intelligence analysts provide "superior wisdom" on any given topic retains a strong hold on our understanding of the political-intelligence nexus. At times, the defense of this "wisdom" has approached incongruous levels. Following the 1962 Cuban Missile Crisis, Sherman Kent wrote a lengthy analysis of the Special National Intelligence Estimate ("The Military Buildup in Cuba") that had, just weeks before the crisis, predicted that Moscow would not send strategic offensive weapons to the island. According to Kent, what the estimate thought would be sound judgment on the part of the Politburo turned out to be precisely that. "In a way," Kent said, "our misestimate of Soviet intentions got an *ex post facto* validation."[16] As Ray Cline, longtime senior CIA official, remarked: "Kent often said his estimate of what was reasonable for the Soviet Union to do was a lot better than Khrushchev's, and therefore, he was correct in analyzing the situation *as it should have been seen by the Soviets.*"[17]

---

ing One's Enemies: Intelligence Assessment Before the Two World Wars (Princeton, NJ: Princeton University Press, 1984) for an even broader account of why expectations regarding intelligence analysis should be tempered. As Robert Jervis, in a review essay of the May volume, noted: "If the historical record is a guide to the future . . . errors will be common. Indeed, it is hard to find cases in which two states, even if allies, perceived each other accurately. The debates over the origins of World War I remind us that even after the fact, we usually argue about the causes of states' behavior and the alternative paths they would have followed if others had acted differently" ("Intelligence and Foreign Policy," *International Security* [Winter 1986–87]: 161).

16. See Kent, "A Crucial Estimate Relived," *Sherman Kent and the Board of National Estimates: Collected Essays*, published by the CIA's Center for the Study of Intelligence. The essay, first published in *Studies in Intelligence* in 1964, was classified "Secret." It can be found at www.odci.gov/csi/books/shermankent/toc .html.

17. Discussant remarks of Ray S. Cline in Roy Godson, ed., *Intelligence Requirements for the 1980s: Analysis and Estimates* (Washington, DC: National Strategy Information Center, 1980), 77. Emphasis added.

I. SHAPING THE FUTURE, NOT PREDICTING IT

Presuming that this kind of Zeus-like judgment is not what we want from intelligence analysts, what then are the implications for the tradecraft of analysis and the relationship between policy and intelligence if we rethink the existing paradigm?[18]

The first thing, perhaps, is to stop thinking of current intelligence analysis as the ugly stepsister to the more edifying work of producing long-range estimates. But such thinking has a strong hold on Washington's mind. From the Church Committee of the 1970s to the panel investigating the intelligence community's failure to foresee the nuclear weapons tests by Pakistan in 1998 to the 9/11 Commission, the complaint has been that the job of providing current intelligence keeps getting in the way of providing high-quality estimates that give policy makers the kind of warning necessary to avoid strategic surprises. But is the trade-off between the resources and attention devoted to current intelligence versus those given to producing longer-term analysis really the problem? Or is the actual problem the unrealistic expectations about what predictive capacities estimates can have? If so, should the failures of the latter really be laid at the feet of the former? And, if not, shouldn't

18. Although Kent's view of the intelligence analyst–policy maker relationship has been the prevailing paradigm for viewing that relationship in the United States for nearly a half-century, it has not gone unchallenged. Early critiques included Willmoore Kendall's review of Kent's book, "The Function of Intelligence," *World Politics* (July 1949), and Roger Hilsman Jr.'s *Strategic Intelligence and National Decisions* (Glencoe, IL: The Free Press, 1956). As Arthur Hulnick noted, Kent himself "was one of the first of the early writers to suggest a need for a conceptual re-evaluation of the Traditionalist theory, because he thought the producer-consumer relationship was becoming unbalanced, and Intelligence was moving away from its relevance to policy-making." However, as Hulnick also points out, Kent's reevaluation only went so far and "could be considered as an attempt to fit Traditionalist theory to practice" (Arthur S. Hulnick, "The Intelligence Producer-Policy Consumer Linkage: A Theoretical Approach," *Intelligence and National Security* [May 1986]: 214).

we accept the fact that policy makers have always wanted, and will continue to want, to be kept abreast of the latest information? Hence, isn't it the analytic community's job to make sure policy makers get the information they want, need, and, at times, have not asked for?

That said, the intelligence community also has to avoid falling into the trap of trying to become the government's CNN. If it is unrealistic for policy makers to expect analysts to predict the future reliably, it is equally unrealistic for policy makers to expect the intelligence community not to get "scooped" by the CNNs of the world. Policy makers might not like seeing events on their office television first or reading about them initially on the Internet, but the fact is, the intelligence community is not really equipped, in terms of global coverage and instantaneous reporting, to compete with the news media. Nor is it clear that it should be.

The intelligence community has a comparative advantage over the media in the area of current intelligence. The intelligence community is able to comment on the reporting as it is received—placing it in context and assessing the reliability of initial reports—and, in turn, to target collection assets to collect additional information that rounds out (or contradicts) the picture being conveyed by the international media. However, neither of these functions can be done instantaneously; during the interim, the CNNs of the world and the Internet will be the principal game in town.

One practical step the intelligence community could take in the face of these realities is to provide senior policy makers with "information specialists." The information specialist would sort through the avalanche of information, spot important items for the policy maker, and be the day-to-day conduit to the intelligence agencies, asking for and receiving from them the required additional data necessary to help fill out a particular picture. Precisely because such specialists come from the intelligence community, they will have better access to specialized intelligence sources and methods, and hence, they will be in a better position to fuse intelligence information with other sources.

To carry out this function effectively, the intelligence officer assigned to this role will inevitably be knee-deep in the workings of the policy shop. He or she will have to know what the government's policies are, what policy options are under consideration, what the adversary is like, and, to some degree, what our own diplomatic and military capabilities might be. Like a scout who goes to watch next week's opponent and reports back to the head coach, the best scouts will have in the back of their mind what their own team's plans and capabilities are so they can properly assess the particular strengths and weaknesses of the other team. The "matchups" are as important as an abstract description of what plays and defenses the other team tends to run. But this means tearing down the "sacred curtain" between intelligence and policy making that still defines so much of our discussions about the relationship. It also requires returning to an older conception of the relationship found, for example, in the role of the G-2 on a military commander's staff. Here, an officer, trained as an intelligence official but under the commander's charge, is charged with collating, analyzing, and briefing all the information coming in to the staff. And precisely because he works on the staff, he will be more familiar with operational plans and his commander's priorities. This, in turn, should give him a better idea of both what to ask for from intelligence and what new intelligence is most likely to have a significant impact on the plans themselves.[19]

---

19. As noted by Robert Gates, one-time head of the CIA's Directorate of Intelligence and later DCI: "Unless intelligence officers are down in the trenches with the policy makers, understand the issues, and know what the U.S. objectives are, how the process works, and who the people are, they cannot possibly provide either relevant or timely intelligence that will contribute to better informed decisions" (Quoted in Roy Godson, ed., *Intelligence Requirements for the 1990s: Collection, Analysis, Counterintelligence and Covert Action* [Lexington, MA.: Heath, Lexington, 1989], 111).

A second implication of this rethinking about the analytic function and its relationship to policy relates to the intelligence community's indications and warning (I&W) function. Put simply, during the Cold War, U.S. intelligence—fearing a nuclear Pearl Harbor—fashioned an extensive and expensive I&W system. This was one surprise no one wanted to face. As best can be seen from publicly available literature, the system seems to have worked well enough when it came to that one issue. Of course, no one knows for sure, because we don't know of one instance where planning for a strategic intercontinental exchange was actually in the works. But what we do know is that we have been surprised sufficiently often enough that the desire to avoid it appears to be more a hope than something to be counted on.

However, precisely because avoiding surprise was, first, so important and, second, an implicit promise of the Kent school of analysis, the tendency has been to look at this issue as though one were a college professor grading an exam consisting of only one true/false question. Were we surprised? If the answer is "yes," then the intelligence community has failed. If the answer is "no," then it has passed. Naturally enough, the bureaucratic response to such a grading system has often been to hide warnings about potential adverse events in a sea of qualifiers or behind obscure language. If nothing happens, senior policy makers will not likely have noticed or cared enough to revisit what they were told; if something does happen, the intelligence bureaucracy will quickly point to that sentence or two—abstracted from the rest of the analysis—that shows they were on top of things.

To end this self-defeating cycle, the analysts and their policy customers have to lower their sights. While the intelligence community should, when it can, tip off policy makers to unexpected events, its principal focus should be less avoiding surprises and more conveying warnings. The goal should be to give policy makers a head's up about those things they should worry about and should possibly take action to head off. Preoccupied senior officials will also need to be given some idea of whether they will likely get any further notice of what might take place before it happens. Again, the measure of effectiveness should not be "Were we surprised?" but "Were we at the appropriate level of readiness?" Policy makers, of course, will complain that this approach might lead to an equally daunting set of problems brought about by a "Chicken Little" syndrome on the part of analysts. Perhaps. But anything that makes policy makers more deliberative is to be preferred to a system that creates incentives for just the opposite.

Finally, if the goal of the I&W system is not to avoid surprise but to warn policy makers of potential dangers in order to spur policy deliberation, it follows that analysts should also consider part of the I&W function to include alerting policy makers of potential opportunities for taking advantageous action. This would require, of course, that analysts be sufficiently close to the policy process to understand policy objectives. As will be explained in the discussion of national intelligence estimates, this could be accomplished by closer contacts through the creation of joint policy-intelligence working groups on specific topics.

A national intelligence estimate is customarily thought to be the most prestigious, most authoritative, most comprehensive, most fully "processed" product of the American intelligence community. It is considered to be the "peak" of the analytic function. NIEs seek nothing less than to explain to policy makers some particular situation of importance by analyzing all the relevant dimensions, assessing the forces at work, and providing some forecast as to how the situation will evolve.

To do so, NIEs must be based on all available relevant data—whether it comes from open sources, clandestine collection, or diplomatic channels—and should be as objective as possible. In other words, an estimate should not reach conclusions designed to promote a given policy or to serve some bureaucratic interest of either its consumers or, for that matter, its producers. Traditionally, this has meant estimates as products of a centralized effort, working under the aegis of the Director of Central Intelligence, who, as the head of the intelligence community, is beholden neither to a policy-making department nor to a particular agency within the intelligence community.

However, these traditional rationales are not nearly as persuasive as they once were. Initially, a centralized effort was thought necessary to solve the so-called Pearl Harbor problem. Without a centralized effort to bring together all incoming intelligence, the likelihood of being surprised would go way up. Yet, in this day and age of computer-supported data banks and networked systems, it is no longer clear that "all-source" analysis for estimates need be done by one entity—be it one team or one agency. And, as already noted, the current estimating system cannot guarantee objectivity. Although objectivity should remain a goal for analysts, there is, unfortunately, no institutional arrangement that can guarantee it.

Moreover, objectivity is not something to be valued in and of itself. The reason we want objective analysis is to provide policy makers with the best information possible upon which they can base their decisions. Thus, the goal should be to make policy makers more deliberative and not give them the pseudocomfort (or, at times, discomfort) that comes from an estimate that typically reflects the conventional wisdom on a given topic. Because every intelligence agency has to work for somebody ultimately, an alternative approach is an increased use of competitive analysis for estimates—that is, a system through which various analytic centers, working for different bosses, develop their own views on the same topic. At a minimum, the resulting debate should make it more difficult for agencies to "cook" their assessments and would alert policy makers to a range of possibilities, which would, it is hoped, sharpen their own thinking.

The downside usually tied to this suggestion is that a policy maker will pick the analysis that fits his or her existing predilections. Yet given the speculative nature of many estimates in any case, there is no reason an experienced senior policy maker will not feel justified in trusting his or her own judgment, regardless of whether he or she is faced with one consensus-driven assessment or multiple competing ones. In short, having one "authoritative" estimate will not fix that problem. What competing estimates can do, if written with rigor and lucidity in the handling of evidence, is force both analysts and policy makers to confront the hidden assumptions driving their own judgments. It doesn't guarantee a wise decision, but it may make the decision more informed. As one longtime senior policy maker remarked: "Policy makers are like surgeons. They don't last long if they ignore what they see when they cut an issue open."[20]

Quite often one hears from senior intelligence analysts that they "owe" policy makers estimates containing their best judgment about a particular issue, even if it is ultimately not founded on hard fact. As Kent wrote in his review of the Office of National Estimate's own misestimate of Soviet intentions with respect to arming Cuba in 1962, given the uncertainties, "[T]here is a strong temptation to make no estimate at all. In the absence of directly guiding evidence, why not say the Soviets might do this, they might do that, or yet again they might do the other—and leave it at that? . . . . This sort of thing has the attraction of judicious caution and an unexposed neck, but it can scarcely be of use to the policy man and planner who must prepare for future contingencies." But, of course, it is. As Kent himself pointed out earlier in his essay, there were a number of other factors—U.S. setbacks in Cuba (Bay of Pigs), the Berlin Wall, and Laos—that could have signaled to Moscow "a softening of U.S. resolve" and led the Soviets to believe that putting nuclear-

20. Quoted in Jack Davis, "The Challenge of Managing Uncertainty: Paul Wolfowitz on Intelligence-Policy Relations," 7. The article can be found at www.odci.gov/csi/studies/96unclass/davis.htm.

armed missiles in Cuba was a risk worth taking. Certainly, any serious policy maker would have wanted to see the possible implications of those factors spelled out in an alternative analysis, especially given the ramifications for American security.[21]

On the whole, the old "Sherman Kent" model for producing estimates, in which intelligence provides input to the policy process from afar, appears too simplistic. Moreover, by aping the natural sciences—that is, by passively looking at the world as though under some microscope—the approach taken by the intelligence community ignores a critical fact of international life today: U.S. behavior. If an estimate is to take into account all relevant aspects of a given issue or situation, what Washington does or doesn't do in any given situation will bear substantially on forecasts of what to expect. To take one old example, the question of whether the regime of the Shah of Iran would fall in the 1970s did not simply depend on what was going on inside Iran. Of no small importance was what the United States might do (or not do) in reaction to the political challenge the Shah faced. Yet, given the wall that is designed to separate intelligence from policy making, factoring in possible various U.S. policy decisions was not thought to be part of the intelligence community's writ. Given the unique superpower status the United States enjoys today, one might expect this problem to have grown more salient, not less.

Addressing this problem probably requires modifying the estimating process so that it becomes an interactive one between the intelligence and the policy-making communities. (In this regard, the estimate process would more closely resemble the British assessment system, in which intelligence analysts are teamed with officials from the Foreign and Commonwealth Office and the Ministry of Defense.)[22] Estimates could, when appropriate, more fully con-

21. Kent, "A Crucial Estimate Relived," 6–7.
22. As Loch K. Johnson noted, "The American end product is an *intelligence estimate*, while the British end product is a much broader assessment that blends

sider U.S. capabilities and options. This would highlight the importance of making the estimators aware of what Washington might
be doing overtly or covertly with respect to any given situation and
taking that into account. In this connection, estimates could make
use of new formats and methods: for example, "net assessments,"
which explicitly compare American and competitors' capabilities
and strategies, or "red teaming," which would analyze potential
strategies that might be used by an adversary to thwart U.S. policies.

Finally, adopting this perspective would bring a healthy dose of
reality to what estimates, in fact, involve—that is, a great deal of
speculative judgment that cannot be reduced to professional, non-
political expertise. Intelligence analysts would retain certain advantages, not the least of which is the time to pull together all available
information on a particular issue and examine it with rigor. But as
important as this advantage may be, it is not a compelling reason
to believe that the expertise and insights of policy makers, diplomats, or defense officials should be excluded when it comes to producing a national assessment on some topic. Indeed, one of the
little-noted findings of the recent Senate Intelligence Committee, in
its report on prewar assessments of Iraq's WMD programs and its
ties to terrorism, was that "probing questions" on the part of Bush
administration officials with respect to the issue of Iraq's ties to
terrorism "actually improved the Central Intelligence Agency's (CIA)
products."[23]

---

the judgments of policy *and* intelligence officers. . . . [T]he British culture actually
encourages commingling, in the belief that the best policy decisions are likely to
result from a pooling of knowledge from among the country's international affairs
experts" (*Secret Agencies: U.S. Intelligence in a Hostile World* [New Haven, CT:
Yale University Press, 1996], 129).

23. Senate Select Committee on Intelligence, *Report on U.S. Intelligence Community's Prewar Intelligence Assessments on Iraq* (July 7, 2004), 34. The report
noted, "Several of the allegations of pressure on Intelligence Community analysts
involved repeated questioning. . . . Though these allegations appeared repeatedly

II. A QUESTION OF IMAGINATION

This essay began by noting how little *The 9/11 Commission Report* had to say about the analytic effort of the intelligence community. Although this is somewhat unusual when it comes to the typical "Monday-morning quarterbacking" that follows most surprise events or attacks, it is not much of a surprise in this instance. The failure to forecast the specific attack that occurred on September 11, 2001, was hardly, or even principally, the fault of the U.S. intelligence analytic community. With no CIA assets inside al Qaeda's leadership to report on its activities and only a smattering of technical collection tidbits of overheard conversations, there were way too few "dots" to connect. Certainly there was enough foreign intelligence reporting over the summer of 2001 to indicate that something was afoot, but probably too little to allow analysts to draw a convincing or even plausible outline of the plot as it existed and unfolded.

Nevertheless, the Commission's implicit argument was that this lack of data might have—perhaps should have—been overcome if a more imaginative analytic effort had been employed to galvanize both the policy-making and the intelligence communities to take seriously the threat we were facing. Whatever the merits of this argument, the Commission's solution treads the traditional path when it comes to understanding intelligence analysis and the estimating process, and it is not a path that will likely arrive at the kind of imaginative analysis they want. To the contrary, one reason the intelligence community had not produced a new NIE on al Qaeda was because, in all likelihood, its own judgment was that things

---

in the press and other public reporting on the lead-up to the war, no analyst questioned by the Committee stated that the questions were unreasonable. . . . In some cases, those interviewed stated that the questions had forced them to go back and review the intelligence reporting, and that during that exercise they came across information they had overlooked in initial readings."

had not significantly changed since the mid-1990s. A request for a new NIE might have raised new issues, but, bureaucracies being what they are, those new points probably would have been buried under a sea of existing views. Breaking paradigms are not what the normal workings of analytic institutions do, nor should we expect them to. Unless they are specifically asked to be a "devil's advocate" or the system is designed to create debate, imaginative products will not be the norm.

Of course, no one system for providing intelligence analysis to policy makers will be perfect. Each has its virtues and its flaws. Over time, any system will be "gamed" by its participants to protect personal and bureaucratic prerogatives. But that prospect is not our current problem. Today's problem is a model of analysis that promises more than it can deliver and is reluctant to come to terms with that fact because such a concession would suggest a less sacrosanct position within the national security system for intelligence analysis.[24] Changing that model is admittedly no small task, as it has been with us for a half-century now. And while concessions have been made here and there to modify the Kent model in practice, a

24. Over the years, intelligence analysts themselves have attempted to come to grips with the gap between the promise of analysis and its actual performance, adjusting the methodologies to reflect a more realistic approach. See, e.g., Douglas J. MacEachin, "The Tradecraft of Analysis," in *U.S. Intelligence at the Crossroads: Agendas for Reform*, Roy Godson, Ernest R. May and Gary Schmitt, eds. (Washington, DC: Brassey's, 1995). (MacEachin was deputy director for intelligence at CIA from 1993 to 1995 and served on the staff of the 9/11 Commission.) Indeed, the training goals of the CIA's Kent school of analysis apparently include efforts to ensure that analysts provide a more nuanced product. Yet, as the Senate Intelligence Committee report on prewar intelligence on Iraq made clear, the basic goal of "clearly conveying to policymakers the difference between what intelligence analysts know, what they don't know, what they think" was never met in practice. (Senate Select Committee on Intelligence, *Report on U.S. Intelligence Community's Prewar Intelligence Assessments on Iraq*, 4–6, 15–18.) Discussions with current officials and members of Congress and senior staff suggest that this remains a problem for much of the analytic product produced by the intelligence community.

new paradigm has yet to take its place, let alone be implemented organizationally.

On December 17, 2004, President Bush signed in to law the Intelligence Reform and Terrorism Prevention Act of 2004, a measure whose genesis arose from recommendations put forward by the 9/11 Commission and whose aim, its supporters claim, is nothing less than a fundamental reordering of the American intelligence community. Whatever else one can say about the act, when it comes to the practice of intelligence analysis, it does no such thing.

The Intelligence Reform Act does, however, contain a number of items that will have an impact on intelligence analysis.[25] What the exact character of that impact will be over the long term is uncertain. For example, the law requires that the new head of the U.S. intelligence community, the Director of National Intelligence (DNI), ensure both that elements within the community "regularly conduct competitive analysis" and that "differences in analytic judgment are fully considered and brought to the attention of policy makers." In addition, the DNI is also required to create analytic "red teams" to challenge existing analytic products. At the same time, the DNI must assign an individual to serve as the analysts' de facto ombudsman, safeguarding objectivity by monitoring possible politicization pressures from policy makers. In theory, these mandates are compatible with each other. But, historically, efforts to create red teams or engage in competitive analysis have been interpreted by the analytic community as a strategy policy makers use to pressure the intelligence community to change its own views on some topic.

One is tempted to say that much will depend on the character and the political courage of the particular DNI—and that certainly will be the case. But, as always, institutions and institutional

25. Intelligence Reform and Terrorism Prevention Act of 2004, PL 108-458, 108th Cong., 2d Sess., Jan. 20, 2004.

arrangements matter as well. They can't help but influence and shape behavior.

Here again, the effects of the changes made by the new reform bill are hard to predict. On the one hand, creating the position of DNI—which, for the first time since the start of the Cold War, will separate the head of the intelligence community and the head of the Central Intelligence Agency—can't help but reduce the agency's dominant sway within the analytic community. As the Senate Intelligence Committee discovered in its review of the intelligence community's performance on Iraq before the war, the CIA and its director "abused" their "unique" positions within the intelligence community to the detriment of the intelligence provided to senior policy makers. While the Director of Central Intelligence is supposed to act as the head of both the CIA and the intelligence community as a whole, the committee found that "in many instances he only acted as head of the CIA." Similarly, the CIA's position as the central repository of all-source intelligence and as the agency that directly supports the director in his role as the president's principal intelligence adviser allowed "CIA analysts and officials to provide the agency's intelligence analysis to senior policy makers without having to explain dissenting views or defend their analysis from potential challenges from other Intelligence Community agencies." In short, centralized intelligence, instead of providing the most accurate and objective analysis to policy makers, "actually undermined" that goal.[26]

On the other hand, creating a DNI—an intelligence czar with real authority over budget, personnel, and intelligence policy priorities—can create a bureaucratic environment that reduces the chances of alternative voices. As Reuel Gerecht noted: "Differing opinions within America's intelligence community would tend to

26. Senate Select Committee on Intelligence, *Report on U.S. Intelligence Community's Prewar Intelligence Assessments on Iraq*, 27–29.

become fewer, not more, as a new bureaucratic spirit radiated downward from the man who controlled all the purse strings and wrote the performance reports of the most important players in the intelligence community."[27] Moreover, charged with being the president's "principal adviser" on intelligence matters, being the head of the National Intelligence Center (the body that produces the NIEs), and creating new "national intelligence centers" to address particular priority issues, the DNI is being handed tools and tasked with responsibilities that appear likely to reinforce analytic consensus and that will do little to enhance analysts' interaction with the full range of consumers within the policy-making community.

In fine, it's possible that the 9/11 Commission's legacy when it comes to intelligence analysis will be much different from what the Commission intends. Rather than promoting the kind of imaginative analysis that it saw lacking within the intelligence community prior to the attacks of that day, the increased centralization of authority with American intelligence they have promoted and lobbied for will actually decrease the chances of it occurring. What may look cleaner organizationally on paper may well be less effective in giving the president and his senior advisors the most accurate picture of not only what is known but also what is not.

---

27. "Not Worth a Blue Ribbon: The Conventional (and Unhelpful) Wisdom of the 9/11 Commission," *Weekly Standard*, August 16, 2004.

3

Restructuring the Intelligence Community

Gordon Nathaniel Lederman

THE TRAGIC EVENTS of September 11, 2001, highlighted two weaknesses in U.S. intelligence and operational capabilities for countering terrorism. First, the U.S. intelligence community could not operate in an integrated manner because its structure was a Cold War relic with no one in charge. Second, the executive branch lacked an effective planning mechanism for counterterrorism operations. These two problems, and recommendations for solving them, figured prominently in the report released in July 2004 by the bipartisan National Commission on Terrorist Attacks Upon the United States.[1] The Commission recommended creating a Director of National Intelligence (DNI) who has sufficient authority over the intelligence community to force integration among its component intelligence agencies and to be accountable for its performance. The

---

1. National Commission on Terrorist Attacks Upon the United States, *Final Report of the National Commission on Terrorist Attacks Upon the United States* (W. W. Norton, 2004) (hereinafter "*The 9/11 Commission Report*").

Commission also recommended creating a National Counterterrorism Center to integrate counterterrorism intelligence activities and
to plan executive branch–wide counterterrorism operations.[2]

Proposals for restructuring the intelligence community by creating a DNI had been floated for decades prior to 9/11, to little
effect.[3] In addition, the Commission's recommendation for a
National Counterterrorism Center represented a virtually unprecedented approach to bridging executive branch departments and
effecting interagency coordination. Only six months later, Congress
enacted and the president signed the Intelligence Reform and Terrorism Prevention Act of 2004 to implement these two recommendations.[4] This chapter summarizes the rationale behind, and the
law's provisions concerning, the DNI and a National Counterterrorism Center. It also responds to common criticisms and offers
some thoughts on implementation.

I. THE GOLDWATER-NICHOLS DEPARTMENT OF
DEFENSE REORGANIZATION ACT OF 1986

The Goldwater-Nichols Department of Defense Reorganization Act
of 1986[5] served as a model for the intelligence reform advocated
by the Commission and enacted by Congress.[6] The 1986 act

2. For the 9/11 Commission's recommendations on intelligence reform, see
The 9/11 Commission Report, 399–428.

3. Richard Best Jr., *Proposals for Intelligence Reorganization, 1949–2004*
(Congressional Research Service, 2004), available at www.fas.org/irp/crs/
RL32500.pdf.

4. Intelligence Reform and Terrorism Prevention Act of 2004, Pub. L. No.
108-458 (2004) (hereinafter "Intelligence Reform Act"). The legislation also covered a wide variety of other counterterrorism topics. This article only deals with
the provisions creating the Director of National Intelligence and the National
Counterterrorism Center.

5. The Goldwater-Nichols Department of Defense Reorganization Act of
1986, Pub. L. No. 99-433 (1986).

6. U.S. Senate Committee on Governmental Affairs, Report on the National
Intelligence Reform Act of 2004 and Accompanying Views, S. Rep. No. 108-359,
108th Congress, 2d Sess. (2004), 5–8.

reformed the organizational structure of the Department of Defense (DoD) in order to foster greater integration among the military services. The services had a history of coordinating their activities on a loose, arm's-length basis. A confederated organizational structure for DoD was arguably sufficient for situations in which the services could fight wars with only limited interaction. However, as the late twentieth century unfolded and technology advanced, warfare required much greater integration across the military services to perform combat operations effectively against sophisticated enemies on a global scale.

Before 1986, however, DoD only had weak mechanisms for achieving integration. For example, the Joint Chiefs of Staff was composed of the heads of the military services and was responsible for providing military advice to the president and the secretary of defense, but its advice frequently represented the lowest common denominator among the services. DoD also had "combatant commands" organized on geographic (e.g., Europe—the European Command) and functional (e.g., military transportation—the Transportation Command) topics and responsible for integrating forces supplied by the military services to fight wars and carry out missions. Prominent combatant commanders have included General H. Norman Schwarzkopf, who led U.S. troops in the Gulf War, and General Tommy Franks, who commanded U.S. troops in the Iraq War. However, these combatant commands lacked effective control over service assets. The resulting lack of integration of service assets produced inefficient and ineffective combat operations.

Congress passed the Goldwater-Nichols Act following a string of military failures in the late 1970s and early 1980s, including the disastrous Iran hostage rescue operation, the tragic bombing of the U.S. Marine barracks in Beirut, and the botched yet successful Grenada invasion. Congress sought to foster greater integration—or "jointness"—among the military services. Of course, Congress could not simply command military officers to "think joint." Instead, it sought to change the military's organizational structure to create incentives for officers to think about issues from a joint perspective—and thus to foster an integrated, corporate DoD culture. For example, Congress elevated the chairman of the Joint Chiefs of Staff, making that official the single, principal military adviser to the president and the secretary of defense; strengthened the authorities of the combatant commanders to make them the preeminent warfighters and the principal figures responsible for fighting wars and performing missions; and required military officers to serve in assignments outside their services to qualify for promotion to general or admiral.

This last requirement in particular led to a sea change at DoD, as the best-and-brightest military officers flocked to serve on the chairman's and the combatant commanders' staffs. By serving on those staffs, the military's best-and-brightest officers not only raised the quality of those staffs but also learned to view DoD issues from a DoD-wide perspective rather than from the viewpoints of their individual services. Twenty years after the legislation passed, the act is credited with having fostered significantly greater integration across DoD, and the notion of returning to a pre-Goldwater-Nichols DoD is essentially inconceivable.[7]

II. THE INTELLIGENCE COMMUNITY'S STRUCTURE BEFORE 9/11

The craft of intelligence has two basic components. The first is collection, in which information about particular intelligence targets is gathered. Collection is done through different methods: human intelligence, meaning spies and informants; signals intelligence, meaning intercepted communications; imagery intelligence; and open-source intelligence, referring to information derived from

---

7. See generally, Gordon Lederman, *Reorganizing the Joint Chiefs of Staff: The Goldwater-Nichols Department of Defense Reorganization Act of 1986* (Greenwood Publishing Group, 1999).

publicly available, rather than secret, sources. The second component is analysis, which involves studying collected information and deriving conclusions, judgments, or predictions. In general, analysis should drive collection so that collection focuses on obtaining the information that analysts need in order to render their conclusions, judgments, or predictions. "All-source analysis" refers to analysis of an intelligence topic using information collected by all relevant methods.

The U.S. national security establishment that fought the Cold War originated in the National Security Act of 1947. That legislation created the National Security Council (NSC), the Director of Central Intelligence (DCI), and what eventually became DoD and the secretary of defense. The Central Intelligence Agency (CIA) was created two years later and was a stand-alone agency, not subsumed within any other cabinet-level department.[8] The CIA was responsible for human intelligence collection and all-source analysis.

In contrast to the CIA, the rest of the intelligence community's membership was located in other executive branch departments.[9] The National Security Agency was created within DoD in 1952 to conduct signals intelligence and to unify the military services' disparate efforts in that area. Another DoD agency, called the National Geospatial-Intelligence Agency, was created to provide imagery intelligence. The National Reconnaissance Office, also located in DoD, procures, launches, and maintains orbiting, information-gathering satellites.[10]

Other entities in the intelligence community include DoD's Defense Intelligence Agency, which supports the secretary of defense, the Joint Chiefs of Staff, and military commanders. The Defense Intelligence Agency does some collection through human

8. Central Intelligence Agency Act of 1949, Pub L. No. 81-110 (1949).
9. The Office of the Director of Central Intelligence was also not located within a department.
10. *The 9/11 Commission Report*, 86–87.

sources, as well as some technical intelligence collection.[11] The intelligence community also includes the national security elements of the Federal Bureau of Investigation (FBI); the State Department's Bureau of Intelligence and Research, which supports State Department policy makers; and intelligence components of the Treasury and Energy Departments.

The intelligence community before 9/11 could be understood as being divided along two axes. The first was the CIA/DoD divide. The CIA—doing human intelligence collection and all-source analysis—was an independent entity, while agencies performing signals and imagery intelligence were located within DoD. The second axis was the foreign/domestic divide. The National Security Act of 1947 forbid the CIA from performing internal security functions. At the same time, the FBI protected its role as the premier domestic intelligence and law enforcement agency. Moreover, the abuses committed by intelligence agencies in the 1960s and early 1970s, chronicled by Congress's Church and Pike Committees, led to an understandable reluctance across the intelligence community to bridge the foreign/domestic divide.

III. THE DIRECTOR OF CENTRAL INTELLIGENCE'S INSTITUTIONAL WEAKNESS

The intelligence community lacked a strong central management structure. The DCI had three jobs: head of the intelligence community, principal adviser to the president on intelligence matters, and head of the CIA. Each, by itself, would overwhelm any single person. In addition, the DCI suffered from an inherent conflict of interest: As head of the intelligence community, the DCI was supposed to make resource and policy decisions for the intelligence community as a corporate unit. But the DCI was also head of the

11. Ibid., 87.

CIA, a component of the intelligence community with its own specific views and interests.

Most important, however, the DCI lacked sufficient authority to manage the intelligence community. Because the CIA is independent of any executive branch department, the DCI had plenary authority over the CIA and did not share control of the CIA with any other department secretary. In contrast, as noted above, the other elements of the intelligence community are resident in other departments, and the DCI had to share authority over those entities with the relevant department secretaries. However, as discussed below, the balance of power was tipped in favor of the department secretaries and against the DCI.

Determining the scope of the DCI's authority and responsibilities requires an understanding of how federal departments and agencies are funded. The standard procedure begins with budget proposals assembled by departments and submitted to the president. The president, with the assistance of the Office of Management and Budget, reviews those proposals and submits the integrated budget proposal to Congress. Congress reviews the president's budget proposal and passes appropriations bills, one for each department or area of government (e.g., the Defense Appropriations Bill for DoD and the Commerce-Justice-State Appropriations Bill for the Departments of Commerce, Justice, and State), that dictate the actual funding for the next fiscal year. Upon passage of the appropriations bills, the Office of Management and Budget apportions the funds, setting a schedule for each department to draw funds from the U.S. Treasury. Each department then executes its appropriation by drawing funds from the Treasury, distributing them among departmental components, and using the funds to pay salaries, buy computers, acquire equipment, and so on.

Despite being the nominal head of the intelligence community, the DCI lacked key authorities that any chief executive officer in the private sector would find essential, including control over the organization's funding, the movement of resources to respond to new priorities, and the hiring of senior managers. His hands were tied in a number of specific ways.[12]

- *Developing the Intelligence Budget:* Under the National Security Act, the DCI had the responsibility to "facilitate the development" of the intelligence budget for consideration by the president and then submission to Congress.[13] This vague language was interpreted in the executive branch as essentially requiring that the DCI and the secretary of defense jointly fashion the budgets for intelligence agencies and programs within DoD, such as the National Security Agency, the National Geospatial-Intelligence Agency, and the National Reconnaissance Office.

- *Executing the Intelligence Appropriation:* In contrast to all other departments, the intelligence appropriation is classified. To keep the amount classified, the funding needs to be hidden in other departments' appropriations. Because most intelligence agencies and entities are actually located in other departments, the result was that the intelligence agencies, aside from the CIA (the only intelligence agency not located in another department), received their appropriated funds directly from their department heads and with little DCI involvement. Thus, the DCI had no responsibility for executing funds for most of the intelligence community's agencies and components, aside from the CIA.

  Without responsibility for executing these intelligence funds, the DCI had little knowledge of how intelligence agencies other than the CIA were actually spending their funds. As a result, the DCI did not know where pools of unspent money were located and, thus, what was available for transfer to higher or

12. Ibid., 410.
13. 50 U.S.C. section 403-3(c), prior to passage of the Intelligence Reform and Terrorism Prevention Act of 2004.

emerging priorities. Moreover, the DCI lacked the leverage over intelligence agencies that comes from being able to control the funding spigot. For example, the DCI could not slow the flow of funds to an agency to discipline it for failing to implement DCI directives or to cooperate with other intelligence agencies.

- *Moving Resources to Meet New Priorities:* The DCI had no unilateral authority to move funds and personnel across the intelligence community to respond to emerging threats. The DCI could only move funds and personnel from an intelligence agency with the concurrence of the secretary of the department housing that agency. And the DCI had no authority at all to move funds and people from the FBI.[14]

- *Hiring Senior Officials:* The DCI had only limited authority over the selection of senior intelligence officials. The secretary of defense was required to seek the DCI's concurrence before submitting a recommendation to the president for the directors of the National Security Agency, National Geospatial-Intelligence Agency, and National Reconnaissance Office. However, the secretary of defense could forward his or her recommendation to the president over a DCI objection, provided the secretary notified the president of the DCI's objection. The DCI had an even lesser role in selecting other senior intelligence officials of other agencies aside from the CIA. The secretaries of the relevant departments merely had to consult the DCI before appointing or making a recommendation to the president regarding the assistant secretary of state for intelligence and research and the directors of the Treasury and Energy intelligence offices. And the DCI had little influence over the selection of senior FBI intelligence officials.[15]

14. 50 U.S.C. section 403-4(d), prior to passage of the Intelligence Reform and Terrorism Prevention Act of 2004.

15. 50 U.S.C. section 403-6, prior to passage of the Intelligence Reform and Terrorism Prevention Act of 2004.

Without control of the purse strings and other key formal authorities, the DCI's power across the intelligence community became a function of the DCI's relationship with the president. In the executive branch, a senior official's close relationship with the president brings enhanced prestige and, thus, greater informal power in internal executive branch politics. As the president's principal intelligence adviser, the DCI theoretically had access to the president. However, the DCI's relationship with the president varied across administrations and by personality. Some DCIs had daily and direct access to the president, while others had only limited access.

The DCI did have some authority "on paper" in the National Security Act that he could have exploited to foster integration and a strong corporate culture across the intelligence community. However, the DCI's lack of authority over funding meant that he had little institutional power to enforce integration. In addition, the DCI's inherent conflict of interest as head of the CIA also dissuaded him from enforcing integration. The net result was that the intelligence community lacked strong centralized management and, therefore, functioned as a loose confederation of agencies—or "stovepipes"—rather than as a single corporate unit.

IV. THE INTELLIGENCE COMMUNITY, THE COLD WAR, AND TWENTY-FIRST CENTURY THREATS

Despite its failure to produce integration, the intelligence community's organizational structure was arguably sufficient for the Cold War, due to the nature of the enemy and the world environment. For more than four decades following World War II, America's principal adversary was a coalition of lumbering, bureaucratic, and technologically challenged nation-states led by the Soviet Union. Cell phones, e-mail, and the Internet did not exist, and events in general flowed at a slower pace as compared with today's "Internet time." The Soviet bloc's main weapon was its military, featuring legions of conventional and nuclear forces and backed by a massive military-industrial complex. The Soviet bloc hid behind the Iron Curtain, keeping as much of its information secret as possible and publicly releasing mainly propaganda. Finally, the Soviet bloc was deterred by the concept of Mutual Assured Destruction: The United States would be able to identify the Soviet bloc as the source of a nuclear attack and respond with devastating force.

The intelligence community's task was to penetrate the Iron Curtain to assess the Soviet bloc's military and industrial assets. It focused on stealing secrets; open-source intelligence was less important. The intelligence community also sought to ensure that the Soviet behemoth did not strike unexpectedly. It knew, though, that a Soviet conventional strike would likely be preceded by a relatively obvious mobilization windup. Given that the targets were slow, bureaucratic nation-states, the intelligence community could operate at a more deliberate speed. Cold War intelligence activity was like a track-and-field meet composed of individual competitions—the pace was deliberate, and each agency could operate with relative autonomy and merely arm's-length assistance from each other. The threat of Soviet espionage also dissuaded intelligence agencies from designing information-sharing links oriented toward rapid transmission. Finally, the conventional, hierarchical, and bureaucratic nature of the target lent itself to a relatively easy cataloguing of who-needed-to-know-what-information within the intelligence community. Agencies shared information among themselves in a slower, more formal, and less intimate manner, dominated by the need-to-know principle.

In addition, the nature of the threat permitted the intelligence community to maintain a sharp divide between foreign and domestic intelligence agencies. Although the United States did face the threat of Communist intelligence activity domestically, it was less grave than the threat of suicidal terrorists bent on mass destruction.

And, as noted above, the civil liberties abuses perpetrated by the intelligence community in the 1960s and early 1970s made the intelligence community of the 1980s and 1990s understandably reluctant to take forward-leaning measures to bridge the foreign/domestic divide. Thus, the foreign-oriented intelligence agencies and the domestically oriented FBI operated with little integration. The foreign/domestic divide rendered the game of espionage like football: Offense and defense were sharply distinguished, and the intelligence community fielded separate squads for each.

But the nature of the threat against America changed dramatically in the 1990s. The world was transformed by the Internet, other advanced communication technology, and the myriad linkages fostered by globalization. Sophisticated trade and transportation pathways spread across the world. International travel became routine. Migration of people and organizations across borders grew easier. As the Soviet threat receded, the Islamic extremist movement, epitomized by al Qaeda, rose. Rather than fielding military phalanxes, al Qaeda dispersed operatives around the world. The 9/11 hijackers, for example, nestled in a variety of places, including a university in Germany and the camps of Afghanistan, and traveled globally. Terrorists could buy off-the-shelf telecommunications equipment cheaply, giving them worldwide instantaneous communications capabilities.[16] They had access to reservoirs of private funding. And, willing to commit suicide in order to attack civilians, they were not deterred by the concept of mutual assured destruction.

As a result of these capabilities, terrorists could strike around the globe with little warning. Bruce Berkowitz called the new threat "a swarming attack," in which

> members of the swarm are interconnected by communications. Each occasionally "pings" its brethren to find out what they are

16. *The 9/11 Commission Report*, 88.

doing and what information they have. . . . [T]hey keep a low profile to avoid detection. When they spot their target, they pounce to attack, possibly simultaneously from several directions or when the target is most vulnerable.[17]

Fighting these new terrorist networks requires the intelligence community to integrate intelligence agencies' capabilities. To have stopped the 9/11 hijackers, the intelligence community needed the agility to have, among other things, discovered Islamic terrorist cells in Germany, Afghanistan, and the United States; tracked individual terrorists as they traveled around the world; penetrated these small groups of Islamic extremists; and extinguished the financial and logistical network that sustained them.

In other words, the intelligence community needed the capability to find, track, and disrupt a handful of sophisticated and networked needles constantly moving through a global haystack. This demands much more intimate cooperation among intelligence agencies than during the Cold War—hence, the parallel with DoD's need for greater integration prior to the Goldwater-Nichols Act. Hunting global terrorist groups is like assembling a giant jigsaw puzzle in which the significance of one piece might not be known until it is arrayed—in real time—against other ostensibly unrelated pieces. Accordingly, at the simplest level, the need-to-know principle became a significant hindrance to effective information-sharing, because the nature of counterterrorism made it difficult to ascertain who needed to know what.

As with the need-to-know principle, the strict foreign/domestic separation that had dominated the intelligence community became more problematic inasmuch as al Qaeda plotted the 9/11 attack abroad, crossed the U.S. border with relative ease, and struck the American homeland from within. In this sense, the intelligence

---

17. Bruce Berkowitz, *The New Face of War: How War Will Be Fought in the 21st Century* (The Free Press, 2003), 102.

game began to resemble less football and more basketball and hockey: fast-paced, rapidly covering a lot of territory, moving back and forth seamlessly between offense and defense—that is, across the foreign/domestic divide—and with little time to field a separate squad or substitute players.

As the 9/11 attacks demonstrated, the intelligence community's loose and confederated organizational structure was unsuited for twenty-first century threats, which required agility and flexibility. In an effort to bridge agency stovepipes, an organization called the DCI's Counterterrorist Center was developed to integrate counter-terrorism capabilities across the intelligence community. However, the Counterterrorist Center never fulfilled this objective. In keeping with the community's domination by agencies, the Counterterrorist Center was subsumed by the CIA and did not emerge as an inde-pendent body separate from any agency.[18] As a result, there was no one below the DCI who had authority or responsibility to mar-shal the intelligence community's capabilities, as a whole, on behalf of counterterrorism.

In December 1998, then-DCI George Tenet issued a memoran-dum stating that America was at war with al Qaeda and calling on the intelligence community to spare no resources in prosecuting the fighting.[19] However, little happened as a result of this directive. The director of the National Security Agency did not believe that the memorandum applied to his agency, while the CIA believed it applied to the other intelligence agencies.[20] And most important, Tenet had limited authority to shift resources within the intelligence

18. Joint Inquiry into Intelligence Community Activities Before and After the Terrorist Attacks of September 11, 2001, Report of the U.S. Senate Select Com-mittee on Intelligence and the U.S. House Permanent Select Committee on Intel-ligence, Together with Additional Views, S. Rep. No. 107-351, H. Rep. No. 107-792, 107th Congress, 2nd Sess. (2002), 339; and *The 9/11 Commission Report*, 353–358.
  19. *The 9/11 Commission Report*, 357.
  20. Ibid., 357.

community to meet an emerging and dangerous threat and to back up his memorandum with resources.

As with DoD before Goldwater-Nichols, greater integration across the intelligence community's capabilities was needed to counter twenty-first century threats. Reacting to the lack of integration and corporate leadership in the intelligence community, the 9/11 Commission recommended dividing the DCI into two separate officials: a Director of National Intelligence with strengthened authorities and a CIA director who was subordinate to the DNI. The DNI would have authority over the intelligence community's funding, movement of resources in response to emerging threats, and selection of senior intelligence officials.

There were several considerations informing this approach:

- *Freeing the DNI to Concentrate on Community Affairs:* Relieving the DNI of responsibility for overseeing the CIA on a day-to-day basis would make his or her workload more manageable and would remove an inherent conflict of interest.

- *Empowering the DNI to Create an Intelligence Network:* The intelligence agencies need to be integrated into a network in which information, people, and resources flow freely and the agencies' capabilities are harnessed synergistically to achieve missions. But creating a network requires common protocols among agencies concerning security, information technology, personnel, and other policies and procedures. The DNI would set those protocols to achieve maximum integration and would have the funding and other necessary authorities to force agencies to abide by those protocols.

- *Concentrating the Intelligence Community on Mission-Oriented Centers:* Integrating intelligence capabilities requires creating National Intelligence Centers that are truly separate from the intelligence agencies and that have the authority to marshal the agencies' capabilities against particular intelligence targets. The National Intelligence Centers would concentrate on transnational and geographic topics reflecting key National Security Council or DNI priorities—for example, the Middle East or East Asia. The model for these centers is DoD's combatant commands—separate from the military services and responsible for integrating the services' capabilities to fight wars and accomplish missions. Only a strong and independent DNI could establish and nurture these centers as entities distinct from the agencies and able to integrate the agencies' capabilities to accomplish intelligence missions. These centers would also decentralize the intelligence community's execution of its missions. No longer would the DCI be the sole point at which all of the intelligence community's capabilities come together against a particular target. Instead, the head of a National Intelligence Center would be responsible for the community's performance against that center's target.

- *Clarifying Accountability for the Intelligence Community's Performance:* The DNI would have sufficient authority to be held accountable for the intelligence community's performance and, thus, would have the motivation to develop communitywide strategies and capabilities to enhance the intelligence community's performance.

As part of its recommendation for creating a DNI, the 9/11 Commission advocated declassifying the top line (i.e., the aggregate dollar amount) of the intelligence appropriation and also the top line appropriation for each intelligence agency.[21] There were two rationales. First, informing the public how intelligence spending compares with spending on other areas would increase accounta-

21. Ibid., 416.

bility. It would also allow the public to get an impression of the intelligence community's relative priorities among different types of collection methods. Second, and more important, declassifying the intelligence appropriation would enable Congress to appropriate the intelligence funds directly to the DNI for distribution among the intelligence agencies, rather than having the funds flow through departmental secretaries to the intelligence agencies within their respective departments. A declassified appropriation would permit the DNI to have clear control of the purse strings and would eliminate opportunities for department secretaries to exploit their control over the flow of funds to try to control intelligence agencies within their respective departments.

V. PLANNING EXECUTIVE BRANCH–WIDE COUNTERTERRORISM OPERATIONS

The Commission's recommendation for a DNI focused on improving the performance of the intelligence community against networked twenty-first century threats. However, the Commission also identified a larger problem connected to counterterrorism that afflicted the entire executive branch. The Commission observed that counterterrorism is a complex and interdisciplinary problem that requires the combined efforts of a wide variety of government agencies. Acquiring intelligence against terrorism is, of course, essential. But so too are many other tasks: military operations for destroying terrorist facilities; diplomatic action for building multilateral coalitions and dissuading states from supporting terrorism; public diplomacy and foreign aid for swaying terrorist sympathizers and giving potential terrorist supporters a greater stake in stability; law enforcement operations for apprehending and incarcerating terrorists; and border security operations for blocking terrorists from entering, and for deporting terrorists from, the United States.

However, there was no mechanism within the executive branch

for ensuring that departments' counterterrorism operations worked under a common strategy and set of objectives. Just as the intelligence community was dominated by the intelligence agencies, the executive branch writ large was dominated by strong departments—with weak mechanisms for cooperation among them.

Without an executive branch body responsible for planning operations, the task fell to the NSC staff. However, that staff was ill-suited to the task. The Iran/Contra Affair of the mid-1980s, in which NSC staffers ran a rogue operation to trade weapons to Iran in exchange for the release of U.S. hostages in Lebanon and to fund the Contra guerrillas fighting in Nicaragua, illustrated the dangers of having operations planned inside the White House. In addition, despite a significant post-9/11 expansion in size, the NSC lacked the staff resources to handle the overwhelming pace of tactical matters associated with counterterrorism operations.[22] Most important, the NSC staff exists to provide policy and strategic support to senior decision makers; focusing on tactical and operational matters distracts the staff from its primary purpose.

The 9/11 Commission's recommendation for a National Counterterrorism Center was designed to remedy the intelligence community's structural problems, particularly the lack of an appropriate entity for performing executive branch–wide counterterrorism operational planning. The Commission conceived of the National Counterterrorism Center as having two directorates. The first would essentially serve as the National Intelligence Center for Counterterrorism within the intelligence community. It would focus on the counterterrorism mission and have responsibility for integrating the intelligence agencies' capabilities against terrorism. It would be the preeminent body for analyzing terrorism and assessing the terrorist threat. It would also establish requirements to guide intelligence agencies' collection activities against terrorism.

22. Ibid., 402.

The National Counterterrorism Center's second directorate would develop plans for counterterrorism operations for the entire Executive Branch and would assign responsibilities for implementation to various departments. By design, though, this directorate would lack the authority to order departments to carry out the plans; that authority would remain with department secretaries.

To give the National Counterterrorism Center the prestige and influence necessary to impel departments to carry out its plans voluntarily, the Commission advocated giving the director of the National Counterterrorism Center a role in the selection of key counterterrorism officials across the executive branch, such as the State Department's ambassador-at-large for counterterrorism and the heads of key military commands that carry out counterterrorism operations, such as the Special Operations Command. In this vein, the Commission also recommended making the National Counterterrorism Center director responsible for reviewing the counterterrorism-related budget proposals of various departments. Due to these authorities, senior counterterrorism officials in the departments would be primed to adhere to the National Counterterrorism Center's plans.[23] Thus, the National Counterterrorism Center would be the beginning of a Goldwater-Nichols for the executive branch— to integrate the executive branch's capabilities to accomplish missions.

VI. THE INTELLIGENCE REFORM AND TERRORISM PREVENTION ACT OF 2004

Congress responded to the Commission's report immediately. The 9/11 Commission received significant media attention during the course of its work due to the importance of its endeavor and to the Commission's series of publicly released staff statements and high-

23. Ibid., 405–406.

profile hearings. Controversy surrounding whether National Security Advisor Condoleezza Rice would testify and the testimony of former NSC staffer Richard Clarke dominated the national stage. Also, the public put pressure on Congress, in general, to act on the recommendations to protect the United States against terrorism, and the presidential election—in which counterterrorism issues were playing a major role—loomed in November. Finally, the Iraq War underscored the intelligence community's problematic performance, even after 9/11. President George W. Bush supported the Commission's recommendations for a DNI and National Counterterrorism Center, in part by issuing executive orders to enhance the DCI's authorities and to lay the groundwork for the center.

Intelligence reform was one of the crown jewels of legislative activity, having been proposed as early as the 1950s but continually running into opposition from departments that would lose some authority over intelligence agencies and from those departments' overseers in Congress. But in a frenetic six-month sprint from late July to December 2004, Congress passed and the president signed legislation that implemented the Commission's recommendations for a DNI and a National Counterterrorism Center, as well as a wide range of other Commission recommendations and counterterrorism measures.

A. Background on the Legislative Process

Following the release of the Commission's report, both the Senate and the House began to draft implementing legislation. The Senate effort was led on a bipartisan basis by Republican Senator Susan Collins of Maine and Democratic Senator Joseph Lieberman of Connecticut. The bill emerging from the Senate had a robust conception of the DNI and described operations of the National Counterterrorism Center in detail. In addition, it created a Privacy and Civil Liberties Oversight Board, which the Senate felt was necessary to balance the risks to civil liberties of a more integrated intelligence structure, and an information-sharing structure across the executive branch. The bill required the declassification of the intelligence appropriation's top-line total and gave the DNI unlimited authority to move intelligence personnel and funds in response to emerging threats without the affected department secretaries' concurrence. The bill also created a series of officials to assist the DNI, such as a chief financial officer, and it established entities within the intelligence community to promote competitive analysis and analysts' independence from politicization. The Senate passed the bill, 96–2.

The House of Representatives took a different approach. Its bill covered a wide expanse of counterterrorism issues, including immigration and criminal penalties. The House characterized its bill as implementing nearly the full range of the Commission's recommendations, although the House bill contained controversial immigration provisions not recommended by the Commission. The House bill also took a more restricted view of the DNI's authorities, kept the intelligence appropriation classified, and provided for only a skeletal DNI staff. It had very little detail about the National Counterterrorism Center but implied that the center's planning directorate would focus only on high-level strategy rather than on operationally oriented issues. Finally, the House legislation lacked a Privacy and Civil Liberties Oversight Board. House Democrats preferred the Senate bill, and the House bill was passed on a generally party-line vote.

In keeping with the standard legislative procedure, a "conference" was held between the Senate and House to resolve differences between the bills. The major issues in the conference included the DNI's authorities and how they affected department secretaries' authorities over intelligence agencies housed within their respective departments, whether to declassify the top line of the intelligence appropriation, the extent to which the legislation should create specific DNI staff positions, the scope of the National Counterterrorism

Center, the creation of the Privacy and Civil Liberties Oversight
Board, the creation of an information-sharing environment in the
executive branch, criminal penalties, and immigration provisions.
The DNI, National Counterterrorism Center, Privacy and Civil Liberties Oversight Board, and information-sharing issues were
resolved, and many controversial immigration provisions were
dropped. The final bill was adopted 89–2 in the Senate and 336–
75 in the House. The president signed the Intelligence Reform and
Terrorism Prevention Act of 2004 on December 17, 2004.

B. Major Provisions

The legislation creates a Senate-confirmed DNI separate from the
CIA director and responsible for leading the intelligence community
and serving as the president's principal intelligence adviser. The
DNI is the same pay-grade as department secretaries (Executive
Schedule Level I). The legislation grants the DNI sufficient authority
to manage the intelligence community and to be held accountable
for its performance. The DNI has several critical responsibilities:

- *Determining the Intelligence Budget:* The legislation states that
  the DNI shall determine the intelligence budget proposal submitted to the President for consideration and submission to
  Congress.[24] Congress understood that the administration would
  interpret the word "determine" to mean that the DNI has sole
  authority, rather than having to gain the secretary of defense's
  concurrence, to submit a budget proposal to the president for
  intelligence that included intelligence agencies within DoD.
  Under the legislation, the DNI may interact directly with the
  intelligence agencies in the formation and submission of their

---

24. Intelligence Reform Act, section 1011, inserting section 102A into the
National Security Act of 1947.

budget proposals, rather than having to go through department secretaries.[25]

- *Managing the Execution of the Intelligence Appropriation:* This area was at the heart of conference negotiations between the Senate and the House. The legislation keeps the intelligence appropriation classified and therefore flowing through departments such as DoD rather than going directly to the DNI. With both the House and the White House opposed to declassification, the Senate was forced to concede. However, the legislation gives the DNI significant control over the funds flowing through the departments to the intelligence agencies. The DNI gives "exclusive direction" to the Office of Management and Budget with respect to the apportionment of funds drawn on the U.S. Treasury.[26] A robust apportionment schedule will serve to curtail a department's discretion in disbursing funds to components within the department, thus preventing a department from trying to influence its intelligence agencies by altering, or threatening to alter, the flow of intelligence funds to them. The legislation permits the DNI to audit and monitor how departments are expending the funds. Departments are required to disburse the funds expeditiously, and the DNI shall alert the president and Congress to any problems caused by the departments.[27] Thus, the legislation gives the DNI leverage over intelligence agencies via control of the intelligence funds.

- *Transferring Funds and Personnel:* These provisions were the other major focus of the conference negotiations concerning the DNI. The DNI does not need a department secretary's approval to move up to $150 million from agencies per fiscal year to meet emerging threats, provided that the funds moved are less than

25. Ibid.
26. Ibid.
27. Ibid.

5 percent of an agency's intelligence funding and that the fund movement does not terminate an acquisition program. Also, the DNI has authority to move personnel during the DNI's start-up phase. In perpetuity, the DNI may transfer one hundred personnel to a National Intelligence Center during the first year after that center's creation without the affected department secretary's approval. The DNI may make additional personnel transfers pursuant to joint procedures agreed upon with department secretaries. The legislation thus deletes the provisions in prior law that a department secretary may veto the DCI's transfer of intelligence funds and personnel and that FBI funds and personnel are exempt from any transfer.[28]

- *Hiring Senior Officials:* The DNI receives strengthened authority to select senior officials. As under prior law, the secretary of defense must seek the DNI's concurrence before submitting a recommendation to the president for the directors of the National Security Agency, National Geospatial-Intelligence Agency, and National Reconnaissance Office. However, the secretary of defense may not forward a recommendation to the president if the DNI objects. The same arrangement is maintained for the selection of the assistant secretary of state for intelligence and research, the assistant secretary of homeland security for information analysis, and other senior officials across the intelligence community with the respective department heads.[29]

In addition, the legislation creates the National Counterterrorism Center and authorizes the DNI to create National Intelligence Centers as the DNI deems appropriate. The expectation is that the DNI will create these centers on geographic and transnational top-

---

28. Ibid.

29. Intelligence Reform Act, section 1014, amending section 106 of the National Security Act of 1947.

ics according to the DNI's and NSC's priorities. A National Coun-
terproliferation Center is also created, but the president may waive
its creation; this discretion is granted because Congress did not
want to tie the president's hands prior to the March 2005 submission of the report of the presidentially appointed Commission on
the Intelligence Capabilities of the United States Regarding Weapons of Mass Destruction.

The centers and other entities that the DNI may wish to create
are housed in an administrative body called the Office of the DNI,
which technically is an independent agency because it is not located
within any other executive branch department or entity. The DNI's
staff is also located in the office of the DNI. There is a Senate-confirmed principal deputy DNI, and the DNI may appoint up to four
deputy DNIs and designate their authorities and responsibilities.
The office of the DNI also has a Senate-confirmed general counsel,
a civil liberties protection officer, and a director of science and technology.

The National Counterterrorism Center has two parts. Its Directorate of Intelligence is akin to a National Intelligence Center for
counterterrorism, responsible for integrating the intelligence agencies' capabilities. The Directorate of Intelligence is the preeminent
body for counterterrorism analysis in the intelligence community
and also proposes collection requirements to the DNI to guide the
agencies' collection activities. The Directorate of Strategic Operational Planning engages in planning for counterterrorism operations across the executive branch. The term "strategic operational
planning" is lifted from the administration's Executive Order establishing a National Counterterrorism Center but is defined in essence
according to the Senate bill. In fact, there were no magic words for
describing the National Counterterrorism Center's planning work,
because it existed in a gray area between high-level strategy and
detailed, tactical planning. As Senator Joseph Lieberman, one of
the Senate authors of the bill, explained:

The legislation defines strategic operational planning to include "the mission, objectives to be achieved, tasks to be performed, interagency coordination of operational activities, and the assignment of roles and responsibilities." Examples of missions include destroying a particular terrorist group or preventing a terrorist group from forming in a particular area in the first place. Objectives to be achieved include dismantling a terrorist group's infrastructure and logistics, collapsing its financial network, or swaying its sympathizers to withdraw support. Tasks include recruiting a particular terrorist, mapping a terrorist group's network of sympathizers, or destroying a group's training camp. Examples of interagency coordination of operational activities include the hand-off from the CIA to the Department of Homeland Security and the FBI of tracking a terrorist as that terrorist enters the United States, or the coordination between CIA and special operations forces when operating against a terrorist sanctuary abroad.[30]

The legislation makes clear that the National Counterterrorism Center has no authority to order a department to carry out a plan, but the legislation buttresses the center's influence so that departments will have incentives to do so. Unlike the Commission, the legislation gives the National Counterterrorism Center director a dual reporting chain: to the DNI for intelligence matters and directly to the president for strategic operational planning issues. The director, a deputy secretary–level official who is confirmed by the Senate, has the authority to make recommendations to the president concerning departments' counterterrorism budget proposals. Thus, the director has sources of influence to ensure that the National Counterterrorism Center becomes a major player in the executive branch. The legislation did not adopt the Commission's recommendation that the director have a role in selecting senior counterterrorism officials across the executive branch.

30. Statement of Senator Joseph Lieberman, *Congressional Record*, December 8, 2004, S11972.

VII. COMMON OBJECTIONS TO THE COMMISSION'S FINDINGS AND RECOMMENDATIONS

The Commission's recommendations for, and the legislation creating, the DNI and National Counterterrorism Center have been subject to a range of criticism. Neither separately nor taken together do they offset the advantages of restructuring.

First, critics argued that the Commission had been reductionist in its focus on intelligence reform. Even if the DCI had sufficient authority and had reorganized and transformed the intelligence community into a functioning network, critics argued, the 9/11 attacks probably would not have been prevented. This is because the intelligence community can never guarantee 100 percent success in stopping terrorists. If the intelligence community had disrupted the nineteen hijackers, al Qaeda might have regrouped and then perpetrated an attack through other means. Indeed, the 9/11 hijackers penetrated U.S. border security and ultimately boarded aircraft carrying box-cutting tools that were permitted by Federal Aviation Administration regulations. Finally, even if the intelligence community had predicted the use of aircraft as weapons, policy makers might have resisted increasing airline safety due to the resulting cost to airlines and passengers.

In fact, many governmental failures, unrelated to the intelligence community, occurred before 9/11. Of course, this does not mean that the intelligence community itself did not fail. Indeed, weakness in other government areas simply means that the need to improve counterterrorism activities is deep and far-reaching. Moreover, good intelligence is critical for other government agencies to achieve maximum success against terrorism. For example, due to the shortage of resources and the desire to minimize disruption to commerce, border security agents need good intelligence in order to concentrate on the most suspicious travelers and packages. Likewise, combating terrorist finances amid the global economy requires pinpoint intelligence regarding terrorist assets, accounts, and donors. To borrow a military phrase, good intelligence is a "force multiplier" because it increases the effectiveness of other counterterrorism activities. Thus, intelligence reform is needed not only because intelligence is one link in the chain of executive branch counterterrorism activities, but also because it is critical for improving the performance of each executive branch activity against terrorism.

A related but important point is that it is unreasonable, if not foolhardy, to expect the intelligence community to stop all terrorist attacks. In sports, even the best defenses are scored upon. And terrorists need only one attack to inflict enormous physical, economic, and psychological damage and achieve spectacular success. However, the fact that the intelligence community will never perform perfectly is not a justification for permitting problems in the intelligence community to fester.

Second, critics argued that merely getting better people would remedy the intelligence community's problems. DCI Tenet's December 1998 "declaration of war" memorandum was offered in evidence. The Commission had viewed the intelligence community's lack of response to this memorandum as emblematic of the DCI's lack of authority over the intelligence community. However, critics could argue that the memorandum's lack of effect was due to DCI Tenet personally not making an aggressive effort to implement his memorandum—by, for example, summoning the heads of various intelligence agencies to demand action. And more generally, DCIs had authorities on paper in the National Security Act that they arguably did not exploit, so why create a DNI with stronger authorities? For example, although the DCI had to obtain the concurrence of department secretaries to transfer funds and personnel in response to emerging needs, there was little evidence that the DCI had aggressively attempted to force the issue.

Good people are, of course, a prerequisite for an organization's success. The most pristine organizational structure will not deliver effective performance if populated with incompetent personnel. However, even the best personnel cannot make a fundamentally flawed organizational structure work satisfactorily on a sustained basis. Most basically, people respond to incentives, and incentives arise from organizational structure. Changing organizational culture thus required changing incentives, which in turn required changing organizational structure. Indeed, the argument that getting better people would improve the organization's performance over the long term had been offered before passage of the Goldwater-Nichols Act—and history has soundly rejected it.

The issue of DCI Tenet's implementation of his declaration of war and the DCI's authorities goes to the heart of whether organizational restructuring was needed. The Congressional Joint Inquiry after 9/11 regarding pre-9/11 intelligence stated that DCI Tenet had been "unwilling or unable" to implement his "declaration of war."[31] It recommended creation of a DNI with strong authorities. However, there was a major difference between "unwilling" and "unable." If "unwilling," then the solution would be to hire a new DCI. If "unable," then the DCI would need enhanced authorities.

The answer to "unwilling or unable" was that both were true. The Commission presented little evidence that DCI Tenet aggressively sought to implement his "declaration of war." The Commission found that DCI Tenet was focused on the CIA specifically, as his management plan for the intelligence community was essentially to rebuild the CIA.[32] But more important, the position of DCI was institutionally weak when it came to running the intelligence community, which was a significant reason why a DCI such as Mr.

31. Findings of the Senate Select Committee on Intelligence and the House Permanent Select Committee on Intelligence Joint Inquiry into the Terrorist Attacks of September 11, 2001, available at intelligence.senate.gov/findings.pdf, 6.

32. *The 9/11 Commission Report*, 358.

Tenet would focus only on the CIA, over which the DCI had supreme authority. Based on the authorities available to the DCI and the prestige associated with that position, there is little reason to believe that DCI Tenet would have been successful if he had tried to implement his "declaration of war" forcefully and to insist on major reallocations of resources across the intelligence community.

Third, critics contended that removing the DNI's responsibility for running the CIA would deprive the DNI of "troops" and make the DNI into a bureaucratic eunuch. Without directly controlling the CIA, the DNI would become like the director of the Office of National Drug Control Policy—the so-called Drug Czar—an official in the Executive Office of the President who is regarded as having little bureaucratic power over how departments actually spend their funds for and conduct counternarcotics activities.

This criticism missed the point of the Commission's recommendation in two ways. The Commission's recommendation was designed to give the DNI authority for managing the intelligence community and transforming it into a network, including authority to control funds and set standards for security, information technology, and personnel. The DNI would control the purse strings over all of the intelligence agencies, be able to task collection and analysis, and set policies and standards. Thus, the DNI would be far different from the Drug Czar, who lacks control of the purse strings of departmental counternarcotics efforts.

Moreover, the DNI did not go from controlling the CIA (as DCI) to controlling no troops. Rather, the DNI would resemble a chief executive officer, who is the clear leader of the corporation but who concentrates on corporate-level issues rather than running a specific business unit. The DNI's time would be ill-spent running CIA human intelligence operations or any other agency's day-to-day operations. But the DNI would be able to reach into any intelligence agency to obtain whatever information the DNI needs. And the DNI would also rely on the new mission-oriented National Intelligence

Centers to assume responsibility for integrating intelligence agencies' capabilities. In other words, overall power in the intelligence community would be centralized in the DNI so that the DNI could then decentralize the execution of missions and operations, led by the National Intelligence Centers.

Fourth, critics worried that the reforms diminished the CIA's status. However, as already noted, the old situation, which involved dual-hatting the DCI as the CIA director, gave rise to an inherent conflict of interest and obstructed the intelligence community's transformation into a network. In addition, the CIA would actually benefit from the creation of a distinct CIA director, because this would provide it with a senior official devoted full-time to its management and improvement.

The likely nature of the CIA's relationship to the National Intelligence Centers is of special interest. The legislation retains the CIA's authority to conduct all-source analysis but also creates the National Counterterrorism Center (with a directorate of intelligence) and authorizes the DNI to establish National Intelligence Centers to do all-source analysis. The National Intelligence Centers would be the primary sites for all-source analysis for their subjects—NSC and DNI priorities—and would propose collection requirements to the DNI so that analysis would guide the intelligence agencies' collection efforts. The CIA's all-source analysis would concentrate on areas for which there is no National Intelligence Center and on subsidiary issues related to the subjects of the National Intelligence Centers, pursuant to a center's direction. Although the CIA as an institution would lose responsibility for all-source analysis on topics covered by the National Counterterrorism Center and the National Intelligence Centers, CIA analysts would likely be populating the centers (along with analysts from other agencies) as part of an integrated community effort. In other words, the CIA would be hiring and training all-source analysts, who then would be deployed to the National Intelligence Centers to do all-source analysis on major topics or would stay within the CIA to retain all-source analytic expertise on other topics.

Fifth, critics argued that a strong DNI would dampen the conduct of "competitive analysis" and thus decrease the quality of intelligence provided to policy makers. As a general matter, "competitive analysis" refers to multiple analysts scrutinizing the same collected information. The objective is to avoid "group think," in which certain assumptions or interpretations take root among analysts and are not challenged. More specifically, "competitive analysis" refers to the formal process by which the major intelligence agencies with all-source analysis capabilities—most important, the CIA, the State Department's Bureau of Intelligence and Research, and DoD's Defense Intelligence Agency—work together to produce national intelligence estimates (NIEs). These documents are landmark documents representing the intelligence community's aggregate knowledge, consensus judgments, and consensus predictions regarding critical national security issues. By virtue of the involvement of various agencies, the NIEs are supposed to avoid becoming hostage to one agency's assumptions and biases.

In fact, the creation of a DNI would not harm competitive analysis and would most likely improve it. The DNI would facilitate analysts across the intelligence community accessing the data collected on a topic by intelligence agencies because the DNI would use his or her authority to set security, information-technology, and personnel standards to ensure information sharing. Moreover, the DNI would likely increase the use of competitive analysis. Clearly accountable for the intelligence community's performance, the DNI would probably want to take whatever steps necessary to make the produced intelligence as accurate as possible.

Thus, the creation of the DNI would not infringe upon the analytic autonomy of the agencies and entities involved in drafting NIEs. Indeed, as noted above, the better connectivity and information sharing throughout the intelligence community as devised by the DNI would allow all participants in the NIE process to be better informed about the issue at hand. Also, the increased integration of intelligence agencies in their collection efforts that would result from the DNI's leadership would produce better collection and thus lead to better analysis and estimates. At the same time, the players in the NIE process would change. The National Intelligence Centers would be preeminent for key intelligence targets and would replace the CIA in the NIE process when the estimate's subject is within that center's purview. The players in the NIE process should be the three entities responsible for all-source analysis—the relevant National Intelligence Center (if any, or else the CIA), the State Department's Bureau of Intelligence and Research, and DoD's Defense Intelligence Agency, plus any other entities, such as the CIA, determined to have appropriate expertise.

Sixth, critics suggest that the creation of a DNI will hurt the warfighters. The military's reliance on intelligence produced by elements of the intelligence community, and particularly the intelligence agencies within DoD such as the National Security Agency and the National Geospatial-Intelligence Agency, has increased dramatically over the past two decades. The advent of "smart weapons" with highly precise and sophisticated guidance systems has increased the need for pinpoint intelligence. In addition, information technology has developed to the level that the military can deploy avenues of broadband connection to carry intelligence to troops in the field, thus further increasing the demand for intelligence. And the military's involvement in complex peace enforcement and counterinsurgency operations, in which the difference between friend and foe is murky yet the human and political consequences of mistaken identity are high, has also increased the military's appetite for intelligence. And, understandably, the military is tempted to rely on assets funded in the intelligence appropriation rather than pay for such assets out of the DoD budget, as the cost of DoD duplicating the intelligence community's assets is very high.

The creation of a DNI with strong authority over intelligence agencies, including those within DoD, would not hurt the men and women in combat roles. As a threshold matter, tactical military assets would remain under DoD's control. The DNI would only control so-called national assets, meaning the assets that serve the president and more than one department—in other words, the assets of the intelligence community. The military's response to that argument, though, was that the military had grown increasingly reliant on "national" assets fielded by DoD's intelligence agencies, namely, the National Security Agency, National Geospatial-Intelligence Agency, and National Reconnaissance Office. Yet the DCI had tasking authority over those assets under the prior National Security Act, so the intelligence reform legislation was only transferring control of them from one civilian official (the DCI) to another (the DNI). Moreover, it would be hard to imagine that the DNI would not make a priority of support to military operations; and if the president's national security priorities dictated that the DNI should direct assets away from supporting military operations, then DoD's complaint would be with the president, not with the DNI. Also, the military stands to benefit from a more integrated intelligence community that can deliver higher-quality intelligence, and the military would know whom to hold accountable—the DNI—for poor performance in intelligence support. In sum, the better product resulting from the DNI's integration of the intelligence community would both aid the military's actual operations and provide policy makers with better strategic information to guide the overall deployment of military forces.

Seventh, critics were concerned that the Commission did not take into account major changes in the intelligence community since 9/11. It is true that the Commission focused its plenary factual investigation on events before 9/11 and up until President Bush's speech to Congress and the nation on September 20, 2001. In contrast, the Commission only conducted a policy-level review of the executive branch's counterterrorism activities after September 20th. However, the Commission's policy-level review did not uncover any changes to the intelligence community's management that forced the Commission to rethink its recommendations. The DCI's fundamental institutional weakness in statute and in practice was not remedied after 9/11.

For example, the post-9/11 creation of the Terrorist Threat Integration Center (subsequently folded into the National Counterterrorism Center) did not alleviate the Commission's concerns about the lack of integration across the intelligence community. The Terrorist Threat Integration Center's mandate—terrorist "threats"—was vague, and that center concentrated only on analysis rather than also on driving collection. The Terrorist Threat Integration Center's creation was a step forward, but that center did not have the preeminence nor did it represent the shift in organizational paradigm as compared with the National Counterterrorism Center and other national intelligence centers.

Similarly, the Commission's recommendation for the National Counterterrorism Center's operational planning function was based partially on the story of 9/11—how the executive branch tried but failed to track two future 9/11 hijackers as they traveled from Asia to the United States. However, the Commission's recommendation was also based on staff-level visits to U.S. posts in the Middle East, Asia, and domestically, which elucidated the disparate nature of counterterrorism operations and the haphazard and duplicative approach to interagency coordination.

Eighth, critics emphasized that structural reform would not solve all of the intelligence community's problems. Of course, structural reform by itself has limitations. It cannot guarantee information sharing and integration, and creating a DNI does not by itself solve problems within individual intelligence agencies. However, structural reform is designed to affect the incentives guiding personnel, with the aim of fostering a corporate, rather than agency-specific, culture. Because he or she is accountable for the intelligence community's performance, the DNI will be motivated to use the new authorities to develop and enforce integration. And, while managing the intelligence community from a corporate perspective, the DNI will be motivated to hold agency heads accountable for reforming and achieving performance from the individual agencies. Ultimately, the legislation creates a performance-based system: The DNI is given sufficient authorities to manage the intelligence community, with flexibility in how to employ those authorities and structure the national intelligence centers and other community entities.

VIII. IMPLEMENTING THE LEGISLATION AND ACHIEVING THE INTELLIGENCE REFORM VISION

Ultimately, the legislation's success depends on the DNI's exercise of authority, set forth in the legislation, to weave the intelligence agencies into a network. Presidential support for the DNI will be critical as the DNI attempts to assert those authorities. In his press conference announcing Ambassador John Negroponte's nomination, President Bush signaled his backing for a strong DNI:

> As DNI, John will lead a unified intelligence community, and will serve as the principle advisor to the President on intelligence matters. He will have the authority to order the collection of new intelligence, to ensure the sharing of information among agencies, and to establish common standards for the intelligence community's personnel. It will be [Ambassador Negroponte's] responsibility to determine the annual budgets for all national intelligence agencies and offices and to direct how these funds are spent.[33]

The DNI must develop the common security, information technology, and personnel policies and procedures necessary to transform the intelligence community into a smoothly functioning network.

33. Press conference.

But the DNI needs to make clear that the heads of the intelligence agencies report to the DNI and that the CIA director does not report directly to the president. Also the DNI should set performance goals and then hold the leaders of the intelligence agencies and of the centers responsible for meeting them.

Numerous questions of implementation will arise: How should the personnel systems of intelligence agencies, and their respective departments, be revamped to ensure that the best-and-brightest professionals serve in the National Intelligence Centers? How many analysts from the CIA's Counterterrorist Center and other intelligence entities should transfer to the National Counterterrorism Center and other National Intelligence Centers? How should differing security, information technology, and personnel regimes across agencies be standardized and melded together? And how should legitimate security concerns be balanced with the imperative of information sharing? The DNI must articulate a strong vision for how the intelligence community should operate as a twenty-first century network or information enterprise and then implement that vision. The DNI should resolve the myriad practical implementation questions that will arise by reference to the principles underlying the Commission's and Congress's vision for a twenty-first century intelligence community: that the intelligence community's corporate interest is paramount; that the National Intelligence Centers should be the community's center of gravity and be staffed by the best-and-brightest intelligence professionals; and that the community must transform itself into—to use President Bush's phrase—a "single, unified enterprise."[34]

Patience will be needed in assessing the net effect of intelligence reform. Organizational culture will not change overnight but only as new professionals are hired and subject to policies that foster a corporate, rather than an agency-specific, mindset. The National

34. Ibid.

Intelligence Centers and other entities will take time to be established. And common security, information technology, and personnel policies will take time to be instituted. The legislation's full results will only be seen one or two decades from now.

Finally, the National Counterterrorism Center director will need strong presidential support so that he or she has the requisite clout to impel executive branch departments to implement the center's strategic operational plans. And the center should be sure to focus its planning not just on operations to attack and disrupt terrorists but also on operations—involving the full range of executive branch tools, including diplomacy, public diplomacy, and economic aid—to eliminate the root causes of terrorism.

4

A New Clandestine Service: The Case for Creative Destruction

Reuel Marc Gerecht

LET US START with an assertion with which all members of Congress and the Bush administration, including the current director of the Central Intelligence Agency, would agree: The Clandestine Service hasn't performed well against the Islamic extremist target. Now let us make another assertion that is harder to prove (few outsiders have had the opportunity to peruse pre-9/11 operational and intelligence-production files at Langley): The Directorate of Operations (DO)—responsible within the CIA for covert operations—performed poorly against all "hard targets" throughout the entire Cold War, if we measure performance by the CIA's ability to recruit or place intelligence-producing agents inside the critical organizations of hard-target countries or groups. In "spookese," these assets are called foreign-intelligence, or FI, agents. The DO had some luck and accomplishment in handling hard-target "walk-ins," foreigners volunteering information to the United States. According to former Soviet–East Europe (SE) division case officers, all of the important Soviet assets we had during the Cold War were walk-ins. They came to us. We didn't recruit them, though occasionally CIA case officers turned would-be defectors into agents willing to commit espionage inside their homelands. The CIA didn't, of course, admit this datum to the Clandestine Service's junior-officer classes—or to anyone else—during the Cold War. It preferred to maintain the fiction that SE case officers, and operatives from other geographical divisions who prowled the diplomatic cocktail circuit, could find and recruit KGB or other Soviet officials willing to provide critical intelligence. But a former chief of the Soviet–East Europe division, Burton Gerber, once confessed that the few Soviets ever actually recruited—and Africa, where race-conscious Russians could feel very lonely, was probably the best hunting ground—had never been valuable.

To my knowledge—and I have spoken to numerous case officers from all of the operations directorate's geographic divisions and from the Counterterrorism Center—the recruitment myth/walk-in reality usually repeated itself against most hard targets the agency faced in the first fifty years after its founding in 1947. This operational hard fact leaves aside the question of whether the walk-ins and recruitments significantly improved our knowledge of the most lethal aspects of our enemies. In the case of the Soviet Union, the answer would have to be yes, certain key agents did provide highly valuable information, though it is certainly debatable whether any asset—even the most prized scientific sources reporting on Soviet avionics—changed the way the West arrayed itself during the Cold War. These assets never snatched victory from the jaws of defeat, but they probably gave air force planners more confidence in the superiority of their weapons and tactics over those of the Warsaw Pact. With respect to Iraq, Cuba, East Germany, North Vietnam, and North Korea, however, the answer appears to be a resounding no. In the case of the Islamic Republic of Iran in the first few years after the Islamic revolution, the CIA probably gets a "C," since former officials and officers of the old regime, who were kept on in the new, occasionally provided illuminating information about the post-revolution Iranian military, particularly in its fight against Saddam Hussein. After 1989, with the end of the Iraq-Iran war, the death a year earlier of Ayatollah Ruholla Khomeini, and the great Iranian "takedown," in which Tehran demolished the CIA's network inside the country, the scorecard on the operations directorate's performance probably wouldn't be passing.[1] Work against America's likely next superpower adversary, Communist-now-Fascist China, would also probably get a failing grade. Case officers to whom I've spoken differ on this point, though none thinks the CIA's operational work against Beijing should get high marks. At least one, an attentive Chinese-speaking ops officer who served in Beijing in the 1990s, believes Langley's Chinese operations are thoroughly penetrated by Chinese counterintelligence. In other words, what the Soviet Union did to us in the 1980s, the People's Republic is doing now.

It is not my intention here to work through the CIA's operational history, focusing on the quality and impact of foreign intelligence provided by agency assets. That task would be enormously valuable for the institution—honest operational reflection is not a strong suit of the CIA and the small cadre of in-house, highly restricted CIA historians. The task would be even more important for outsiders, particularly for officials and staffers in the executive and legislative branches who are charged with overseeing and paying for Langley's work. The CIA's New Testament motto, "And ye shall know the truth, and the truth shall make you free," is obvi-

1. For the best press commentary on the Iranian "takedown" and for the most insightful journalism on the travails of the post–Cold War Clandestine Service, see John Walcott and Patrick Duffy, "The CIA's Darkest Secrets," *U.S. News and World Report*, July 4, 1994. Although not without its inaccuracies, Walcott's and Duffy's reporting is easily the finest piece of mainstream journalism ever on the systemic problems of agency espionage operations.

ously essential for a functioning democracy, particularly for its
secretive organizations that do not regularly benefit from the intru-
sive light of curious (well-meaning) outsiders. It is consistently
astonishing to see how short the memories are of our elected representatives and their professional staffers. The CIA, whose case
officers rarely read large active operational files, let alone defunct
ones stored in the archives, nevertheless usually runs rings around
White House or congressional officials who attempt, ever so gently,
to query the agency about operational performance. Even senior
staff at the White House don't want to know much about CIA
sources and methods, for fear they could be blamed for revealing
the identity of an agent or the existence of a sensitive operation.
Truth be told, most members of Congress's intelligence oversight
committees really don't like doing oversight.

Critical oversight is, by definition, adversarial, and most congressional members, Republican and Democrat alike, would much
rather be collegial with each other and with the intelligence community—the natural patriotic reflex works in favor of the status quo.
The hidden and massive world of classification also protects the
agency against a vigorous congressional inclination to assess the
bang-versus-buck value of America's clandestine human intelligence collection efforts. Furthermore, the paltry sums involved in
funding the Clandestine Service have unquestionably encouraged a
lackadaisical, trusting approach. But this is not to say that the Clandestine Service is underfunded. Some have argued that the DO's
human intelligence collection—also known as HUMINT—is deficient
in part because the United States spends too much money on technical intelligence. Those critics are, to put it politely, misinformed.
When exuberantly funded—as HUMINT was in the 1950s, 1960s,
1980s, and post-9/11—the Clandestine Service is inexpensive to
maintain. Yet the quality of HUMINT against hard targets that did
not derive from walk-ins was mediocre to awful in the past and,
according to active-duty officers, awful to nonexistent today. I have

never met a case officer who has said, "I couldn't do this important operation because I didn't have the money." Not once. A few billion dollars goes a *very* long way in covert affairs. The agency, like any other bureaucracy, will always plead for more cash, even when operatives in the field have more money than they know what to do with.[2]

The Republican dig at Democratic presidential candidate Senator John Kerry, who pre-9/11 often voted against more money for the CIA, may have been politically astute, but on its face, it made no sense (to be sure the senator has never given any hint that he's grasped the real, nonpoliticized troubles of Langley). Would that more Republicans understood that more money for the CIA is more often than not the equivalent of giving crack to a heroin addict. In fact, the CIA has *always* feared the critiques coming from the American Right more than those from the American Left because the Right has usually focused on Langley's competence, not its operational ethics. A malevolent or "rogue" CIA has to be, by definition, a somewhat competent organization. In my experience, Republican staff members of the two intelligence oversight committees are more likely to approach the agency with greater skepticism and probing queries. Before 9/11, the only staff director of the Senate

---

2. Former CIA director George Tenet, politically the most astute director since Richard Helms, has probably been the most accomplished practitioner of the "If I'd only had more money" CIA school of congressional operations. When Tenet kept doing this line in 2004, after substantial post-9/11 increases in the agency budget, even the traditionally friendly ground of the Senate Select Committee on Intelligence, where Tenet once worked as the staff director, turned hostile and more openly dismissive of his promises. It is, however, an excellent bet that the Senate and House intelligence oversight committees will continue to give the CIA, particularly the DO, more money even though senior members of those committees may question the bang-versus-buck results. No one on the Hill wants to be accused of shortchanging American intelligence in the war on terror. During the Cold War, Democratic Senator Patrick Moynihan often trenchantly (sometimes unfairly) critiqued the CIA's intelligence collection and analysis. Yet Moynihan *always* ended up giving the CIA the monies it asked for.

Select Committee on Intelligence who ever tried to use the committee to push aggressively for a reform agenda inside the CIA and the
broader intelligence community was a Republican. Taylor
Lawrence, a poor Southern boy with a Ph.D. from CalTech, had the
self-confidence to challenge accepted practices in the late 1990s,
when it was crystal clear to him and several other professional staff
members that the Clandestine Service, among other American intelligence institutions, was in trouble. Too controversial for the intelligence bureaucracies and the always-collegial but stubbornly
political Senate oversight committee, he failed and resigned—and
the reform agenda went with him.

The constant refrain one regularly hears on the American Right
that Bill Clinton destroyed, or greatly accelerated the decline of, the
CIA is another unfounded critique. The Clandestine Service was a
mediocre organization long before Clinton's election. Indeed, President Clinton's first director, James Woolsey, attempted to force the
DO to develop standards to review the quality of agency assets—
the first time any director had done so. Senior management and
the rank and file of DO, however, quickly diluted in practice Woolsey's guidelines so that the old habits of recruitment and intelligence exaggeration and fraud continued.[3]

---

3. Woolsey made a similar bold attempt to force the declassification of
defunct covert-action programs. Here, too, the bureaucracy didn't zealously com-
ply. The 1953 CIA/MI6-sponsored coup d'état against Iranian prime minister
Mohammad Mossadeq is an excellent case in point. A brief agency in-house history of this affair should have been quickly released. Langley had in its possession
no other official recollection of the event. Nonetheless, the history remained classified. When this compilation ended up in the hands of the *New York Times* in
2000, the CIA Publications Review Board, according to an official in the review
office, was furious. It had no right to be furious. The declassification folks at
Langley were either negligent or in willful disregard of Woolsey's directive—or
both. After the *Times'* publication, Woolsey remarked to me that his directive was
intended specifically for this kind of historically rich documentation. One would
be hard-pressed to find a more historically resonant covert action. It is possible
the politically incorrect nature of this project may have had something to do with
the institution's disinterest in declassifying it. Given the secrecy temperament,
the bureaucratic depth, and the ahistorical ambiance of Langley, it would be

The standard critiques miss the mark. There simply is no such thing as a case officer who didn't try to recruit a Middle Eastern terrorist because of concerns about the possible legal blow back from associating with someone who may have engaged in criminal behavior. In addtion, the press, retired case officers wanting to underscore their own hard-nosed credentials (and a history depicting the CIA as a more manly, competent place when they were "hitting the streets" as operatives), and a wide variety of folks on the right often can't resist putting the blame for the agency's many recent failures on an American overemphasis of technical intelligence at the expense of HUMINT, on politically correct human-rights sensitivities that mushroomed under Clinton, or on insufficient funding during the 1990s. In fact, these critiques are in no way justified by the intelligence reports, operational files, and firsthand experiences of the young case officers (those who did fewer than four tours) in the Reagan, Bush père, and Clinton years.[4]

---

unwise, however, to suggest too strongly that the CIA was resisting declassifying something that, in today's light, might seem embarrassing. More likely, CIA officials, not wanting to offend their British colleagues, who operate under the draconian British Official Secrets Act, ignored Woolsey's order. According to a historian in the CIA, the Review Board gave greater weight to British concerns than to the statutory authority of a CIA director to determine classification and public access. One thing is certain: Since its publication, there hasn't been the slightest hint of blow back against any Iranian or his descendent mentioned in the official history—the oft-used reason for why the clandestine service refuses to release its past even when CIA directors order it do so.

4. Senior DO officers at headquarters and in the field could, however, be fearful in their approaches toward dangerous targets. According to several case officers, countersurveillance teams deployed to protect operatives in meetings with possibly dangerous foreign agents and "developmentals" became more common in these years. Aggressive counterterrorist officers in the 1980s and 1990s could regularly encounter stiff resistance from headquarters or station management if suggested operational actions were too muscular (must never physically intimidate the other side) or likely to put an officer into harm's way. I can't recall of a single instance where a case officer died because he put himself into harm's way in a clandestine relationship with any terrorist organization. According to several CIA officers, no case officer has died since 9/11 in a clandestine operation against the Islamic terrorist target.

The principle problem during Clinton's presidency, as before
and after, was the inability of case officers to meet Islamic terrorists, those who associate with Islamic terrorists, or even those who
might remotely know those who associate with Islamic terrorists.
In the Clinton era, under directors Woolsey, John Deutch, and
George Tenet, case officers would have loved to be morally and
legally challenged by the possible recruitment of a terrorist who
might have had something to do with the death of an American
citizen. Neither they nor in all probability the directors above them
would have hesitated to move on such cases if there *had been* such
cases. Clinton may not have cared all that much about the intelligence business—though he certainly gave the impression of having
a rapidly growing interest after the embassy bombings in Africa in
1998. But Clinton's weaknesses in foreign affairs mattered not at
all to counterterrorist case officers "on the street."

Read the press commentary on the CIAs of William Casey,
James Woolsey, John Deutch, and George Tenet, and the well-being
and ethos of these institutions look remarkably like what the press
sees as the character of the director. There is a powerful hierarchical disposition in Washington, in both the government and the
press, to judge a bureaucracy first and foremost by the men and
women who lead it. This approach can have merit, particularly
when dissecting institutions where there is an organic relationship
between the leaders and the led—for example, in the military. In
dealing with the CIA's Clandestine Service, however, it makes
almost no sense. I had considerable admiration for William Casey,
the determined, covert action–loving cold warrior. But when he was
the director of central intelligence, Casey was irrelevant to the Clandestine Service's espionage ethics and the vast majority of espionage operations. Even with covert action where CIA paramilitary
officers were not directing recoilless cannon-loaded needle-boats in
the bays of Nicaragua, the influence of Casey was often *very* hard
to detect. The bureaucracy dominated. In seven years of Iranian

operations, at a time in the 1980s and 1990s when Iranian operations often had the limelight inside the service, I'm hard-pressed
to recall a single espionage operation that was shaped by a CIA
director.

Serious historical reviews of clandestine intelligence collection
against the Soviets, Chinese, Iraqis, Iranians, Egyptians, Cubans,
French, or Congolese might make insiders and outsiders wiser
about the nature of the CIA and keep White House and congressional officials from heaping praise on past or present agency work
that does not merit it. As a former case officer, I can say that such
praise was very dispiriting to officers—particularly during the
1980s and early 1990s, when egregious operational failures
occurred regularly. What such officers wanted was outsiders to
reprove the organization for its incompetence. That way our elected
representatives *might* be less inclined to throw even more money
at Langley each time it cocks up. Even if congresspeople or deputy
national security advisers did not read these reviews—and these
folks don't have much reading time—the critiques would still bubble
through the bureaucracy and the press, engendering more healthy
skepticism and humility.

But my objective here is different. I bring up the deficiencies of
the past only to underscore the most urgent problems that now face
us in constructing a CIA that has as its primary target Islamic
extremist groups. Langley properly has a larger role than this—and
I will discuss that role below—but a CIA that tries to reconstruct
itself to battle al Qaeda and other Islamic militant organizations will
surely become a better intelligence service against the Chinese,
North Koreans, or Russians. As is the case with infectious disease
doctors fighting AIDS, agency operatives building a Clandestine Service capable of penetrating Islamic radical groups are learning skills
and operational truths applicable to any hard target. And if the
Clandestine Service cannot wage intelligent efforts against hard tar-

gets—something it has not often done in the past—then it really doesn't have a particularly compelling reason to exist.

What does the CIA have deployed against al Qaeda and other Islamic extremist groups overseas? According to active-duty CIA officers, the methodology of agency deployment today is essentially unchanged since September 10, 2001. Traditional stations and bases lightly camouflaged inside official U.S. facilities are responsible for most of the "street" work—that is, case officers posing as fake diplomats are the overwhelming bulk of the organization's frontline force. Needless to say, this "cover" is nearly useless in working the Islamic militant target. Diplomats and case officers are monitored in many Arab countries, and in serious countries with active Islamic militant organizations and competent internal security services—for example, Egypt or Jordan—any attempt to associate with Muslim activists would be noted almost immediately and viewed hostilely by the host government. The same would be true in much of western Europe, the launching platform of 9/11 and probably still the home of potentially the most operationally effective hard-core jihadists. This issue has greatly retarded the State Department from making contact with Islamic activists. Ditto for undeclared American case officers, who most likely are "blown"— known—to the host government in serious counterintelligence countries like Egypt, Jordan, or France. It is extremely difficult for agency officers, even with real, substantive, full-time State work to long maintain their cover against local employees—State calls them "foreign service nationals"—who dominate the administration in all embassies and consulates in the Middle East and Europe.

An agency officer under diplomatic or consular cover trying to associate with Islamic militants could also easily anger his official State "cover boss," who could get scolded by the Foreign Ministry for allowing one of his officers to go where he ought not. It isn't unlikely that the protest could come through the "host" security service. In either case, CIA chiefs of station are usually loath to anger senior American diplomats or the local security service, which can demand that station chiefs depart their posts. Senior CIA personnel abroad are inevitably married with kids, and they truly fear being declared persona non grata—to be "PNGed" is a dreaded verb at Langley. Quality of life is good for senior CIA officers, even in rather miserable Third World posts. The only way CIA officials can really save money given their low official salaries is to live abroad, where their rent, utility costs, and other day-to-day expenses are covered by Uncle Sam. Chiefs of station, who rule all U.S. operations within their countries, usually take a dim view of case officer activity that has a high probability of getting the station into trouble with the "host" service.

In the future, this problem of militant association may, just possibly, change, depending on how forcefully the Bush administration pushes its democracy-advocacy programs in the Middle East. If Washington were to go to the mat, demanding access to Islamic activists for U.S. diplomats, it might be conceivable that agency officers could occasionally get the opportunity to say "hi" to Islamic militants, though they would likely be constantly or periodically surveilled while doing so. Needless to say, this kind of access isn't particularly helpful, even if the officers concerned have good knowledge of Arabic and the right higher education to converse productively with Islamic activists (and according to CIA officers working on the Middle East, the number of operatives currently serving who have such qualifications is few). Islamic activists come in many different stripes, and it would take considerable time for a talented case officer with unrestricted, unmonitored access to get some idea of the concentric social and intellectual circles connecting moderate Islamists with the harder core ones who might have valuable information about militants who are or could become operationally active anti-American jihadists in the Middle East, Europe, or the United States.

It is possible to dream up scenarios where "inside" State

Department–covered case officers could gain useful access to militant anti-American Islamist organizations: A case officer with consular cover meets a young Muslim male applying for a visa to study in the States and uses the consular leverage for repeated meetings. The young man volunteers information suggesting knowledge of radical Muslim circles, and the case officer recruits him with money and the undefined (and easily forgotten) promise of aiding him later to get to the United States. The young man then proves a valuable access agent cum would-be radical Muslim, developing good information on local al Qaeda membership, recruitment methods, and liaison relationships between radical Muslim groups and the host country's security service. This scenario is certainly possible, which is why consular-covered CIA case officers are essential tools in operations targeting Third World radical organizations. (Radical Muslims with European passports, however, do not need to apply for visas at U.S. consulates, as they may travel to the U.S. on the visa-waiver program.)

America's counterterrorist program cannot be built, however, on the random luck of CIA officers in U.S. consulates. The chances of the above scenario happening are small, though sufficient enough to ensure that all consulates in the Middle East and in other countries with large Muslim, especially Arab, populations have CIA officers inside the consular cadre—not just waiting in the wings and depending on State Department personnel to do the initial spotting and assessing of possible targets. (Consular officers are among the most overworked members of the Foreign Service, and they absolutely don't need to be tasked with security concerns that aren't properly their own.) European and African countries with substantial Arab communities—whose members may lawfully carry several passports—must have well-integrated CIA officers working and reviewing the nonimmigrant and immigrant visa lines—something that, according to active-duty case officers, is rare overseas today, despite the consular/security discussions provoked by 9/11. The

CIA has generally viewed consular cover as a backwater—the work is demanding, and few case officers want to exert such effort on behalf of the State Department when the odds of a recruitment are so small. Case officers, whatever their target, usually prefer the more prestigious, though usually even less useful, State Department political cover to "camouflage" their activities.

The problems of time-on-target and association plagued agency officers in the Cold War on most difficult but conventionally accessible targets. It is imperative for outsiders to understand the depth and surreality of these long-standing problems to appreciate how defective and self-delusional the Clandestine Service has been since espionage replaced covert action as the mainstay of its ethos in the 1950s. If you understand the mind-set and the routine methods during the Cold War, you will understand why Langley has so far successfully resisted pro-reform outside pressure and soul-scorching internal reflection since 9/11. Five decades of mostly bad habits, seen inside as the approved playbook for routine espionage operations, has made the Clandestine Service nearly impervious to criticism and internally driven reformation. Know the truth behind routine Cold War era operations—that they most often made no sense whatsoever—and you will also understand why only massive reform has any chance of changing the debilitating practices of the agency's Directorate of Operations. If, however, you think that the DO did a decent job during the Cold War—and this is the preferred historical starting point for the CIA, which most establishment liberals and conservatives assent to with little hesitation—then it's possible to believe that the agency can adjust to a post-9/11 world without that much internal bloodletting and trauma. Case officers are, after all, Americans, so this theory goes, and they thus will honestly cross-examine themselves for the good of the country. But see the past accurately, and you will understand that Americans, like everybody else, can, in closed societies, continuously and effectively lie to themselves. Gradual change at Langley is no change at all.

So let us take another look at the past before we try to construct a new Clandestine Service. From the 1950s forward, the same scenario played out thousands of times, with case officers trying to target difficult but accessible targets. Consider France and South Africa (but one could just as easily consider other countries in Europe, the Middle East, Asia, or Latin America). I've picked these two countries because they don't represent nearly impossible targets—such as Soviets, North Koreans, Iran's Revolutionary Guard Corps, or Saddam Hussein's security and intelligence organizations, but they were nonetheless very difficult. A decent argument could be made that the CIA should not have spent much, or any, time trying to recruit sources in Cold War France or Boer-dominated South Africa, because both countries were democracies and, as such, revealed enough of their political souls and machinations for Washington to know more or less what they were doing. Both countries, whatever their obstreperousness and moral transgressions, were definitely not on Moscow's side.

Yet these targets were at least more important than the ones that occupied the time of most case officers in most countries. If what the CIA was doing in Paris or Pretoria could look silly, what Langley was doing elsewhere could look absurd. The remark of a senior Africa Division officer who questioned whether a junior officer needed to recruit twenty agents in his first year in a small, poverty-stricken west African state, when "five or six would have been quite sufficient," captures well the gluttony of agency work in easy hunting grounds where case officers could announce their CIA identities and watch a queue develop. In the macho, conspiratorial lands of Latin America, working for the CIA could be a rite of passage. In the Middle East, this same macho-mercenary-join-the-ruling-cabal attitude could also, depending on the country, play to your advantage. The former case officer Robert Baer wore his CIA identity like a multicolored strobe light: He could occasionally pick up worthwhile intelligence from Middle Easterners who wanted to have their own private channels to Washington. (This is not to suggest that Bob Baer wasn't also fun to be with, more fun than the often zealously conventional Americans who predominate in the Clandestine Service.)

Several case officers have told me that when "developing" Cold War Frenchmen and South Africans, the officers could at least pretend they were doing something worthwhile. Unlike the seldom-seen Soviets and Communist Chinese, they could at least wine and dine these targets with greater regularity. But knowing why individual case officers and the Directorate of Operations chased various targets isn't important now. Knowing the structure and method of standard agency operations then is important, since past practices still define the service. The agency's fight against bin Ladinism will continue to be more myth than reality because Langley cannot escape these deficient, though easy, tactics. Never in public, and rarely in private, can senior agency officers, who, after all, attained their in-house "glory" in a thoroughly defective system, admit that these practices failed.

But what follows, boiled down to its basics, is a nuts-and-bolts description of the Cold War agency at work. There were differences here and there. "Denied-area" operations—that is, what occurred behind the Iron Curtain and in other countries where case officers confronted totalitarian security services or where the environment was considered too hazardous or politically impossible for CIA stations and bases to operate—do not involve case officers "on the street . . . developing" foreigners. But what follows is what happened when the Clandestine Service was trying to be serious against what it considered serious, accessible targets. The agency that gave us this charade, the mid- to senior-grade officers who sustained it, are the folks who today are supposed to penetrate radical Islamic groups who would, if they could, detonate weapons of mass destruction inside the United States.

The debilitating, mundane past: An American operative under diplomatic cover in Paris or Pretoria, who had access to select French or South African officials at their respective foreign and defense ministries, had an impossibly difficult time gaining ministry-wide access because the diplomatic cover had to fit established work assignments and patterns. A case officer cum diplomat working the Asian portfolio couldn't just wander off and start paying house calls on foreign counterparts working, say, Soviet or European issues once the case officer discovered that his primary counterpart was a faithful Frenchmen or South African, not at all interested in an extracurricular relationship with the CIA. Real American diplomats could get very mad if they found CIA officers poaching beyond their assigned domains, which CIA officers would regularly try to do, because the odds would be infinitesimally small of finding a diplomat willing to engage in espionage on behalf of the United States in the exact foreign ministry office to which the case officer would have cover access. And expanding the pool of possible targets rarely much increased the odds of a recruitment of a serious first- or second-world official. Frustrated case officers were advised to troll any nonofficial locale imaginable to compensate for the lack of workable official access. "Just sit in the cafés and bars nearest to the foreign and defense ministries and try to meet people" was the *serious* advice given by a performance-award winning senior operative to a hapless, quintessentially American junior case officer tasked to recruit European officials.

Ambitious case officers with "integrated" State Department cover would often just abandon their diplomatic portfolios and hunt anywhere they could hope to find someone "recruitable."[5] It was

5. For press commentary on post–Cold War CIA operations in France, see Edwy Plenel, *"Paris dénonce l'espionnage de la CIA en France," Le Monde*, February 23, 1995; Laurent Zecchini, *"Les États-Unis démentent avoir espionné en*

not at all uncommon to find rapidly promoted officers with a long string of recruitments whose access to power and classified information was at best marginal. Such officers often developed into a fine art form intelligence reporting that oh-so-slightly advanced the political coverage of the local press, which inevitably made agency reporting read like State Department telegrams, except not usually as soundly sourced or as well written. Among the 10 percent of the case officer cadre that has always done 90 percent of the recruitments—in other words, the leadership of the Clandestine Service—the malady of these "cheap recruitments" has been endemic.

The above frustrations were less when CIA case officers would spot, assess, and try to develop these targets and others outside of the foreigners' home countries. Such "targets of opportunity" worked at their embassies or consulates. Professional etiquette and formalities were more flexible—a sophisticated officer could more easily associate with a wider variety of official nationals of another country—but problems of prolonged association often remained. The odds of finding somebody *serious* who was willing to engage in espionage on behalf of America still remained quite small. Hence, again, the need to recruit foreigners of less value. Thousands of such assets have been put on the books. My personal favorite—and

---

France," *Le Monde*, February 24, 1995; Craig R. Whitney, "French Official Demands Inquiry on Spy Leak," *The New York Times*, February 24, 1995; Tim Weiner, "CIA Faces Issue of Economic Spying," *The New York Times*, February 23, 1995; Weiner, "CIA Confirms Blunders During Economic Spying on France," *The New York Times*, March 13, 1995; and "CIA Spying in France," editorial in *The International Herald Tribune*, February 24, 1995. I've spoken to several CIA officials who had knowledge of the "Paris flap," including a conscientious official in the Inspector General's office. They all described the mishap as a perfect storm of recruitment-hungry, dishonest case officers, poor tradecraft, and consistently bad operational judgment on the part of several CIA station chiefs. Press reporting on the affair tended to depict the agency as engaged in serious stuff gone awry, which certainly can happen in espionage. The opposite was true: It was worthless case officer busy work caught red-handed by the politically opportunistic bad boy French interior minister, Charles Pasqua.

it is enormously difficult to choose among the dozens that I gained knowledge of while working two geographic divisions and their corresponding headquarters' desks—was an Iraqi hotel clerk recruited in a European country during the first Gulf War. The agent was recruited as an "access agent" to Iraqi officials, though the asset appeared to have contact only with backpacking American and European tourists. Headquarters actually issued a commendation to the recruiting officer, who would have had some difficulty locating Iraq on the map, for his contribution to America's war effort. A cash bonus followed. (A review of citations, awards, and cash bonuses given to agency officers and stations during the first Gulf War would be an eye-opening voyage through the Directorate of Operations.)

Imagine a Russian diplomat, periodically under FBI surveillance, wandering the halls of the U.S. Senate buildings trying to find a valuable congressional employee willing to commit espionage on behalf of Mother Russia and you can have a different perspective on traditional CIA operational methods for most "unilateral" case officers (operatives who are not openly declared to the "host" security service). Spying for America is admittedly more morally appealing than spying for Russia, but the home-country patriotism working against America in states with profound cultural identities has always been problematic, and with the collapse of the Soviet Union, the appeal of the United States to Western-oriented foreigners as a bulwark against Communism and Soviet malevolence has vanished. During the Cold War, the CIA could never intellectually and operationally come to grips with the global incongruity of its massive "inside" case officer deployment and cover and the true paucity of valuable foreigners susceptible to recruitment pitches by CIA officers. Any attempt to assess this disconnect—to have a thorough historical review, target by target, of the gross number of case officers deployed and the quality of intelligence collected from recruited assets—could have possibly brought the entire house down. Cynicism is rampant in the CIA's Clandestine Service, as it appears to be in other Western intelligence services, in great part because the reality of intelligence collection is so vastly less than its promise. The British author John Le Carré, a former intelligence official, may be a morally purblind, mean-spirited left-winger, but he often captures well the cynicism that comes with the trade—the intensity with which case officers can despise their own dishonest organizations.

In the CIA of Porter Goss, the "head count"—the need to show recruitments or progress toward recruitments for a case officer's annual performance report—remains the most assured way for rapid case officer promotion. The CIA tenaciously denies that agent recruitments—"scalp counting"—is *the* key to success and that case officers engage in "cheap recruiting." When I first wrote about this debilitating problem in the *Atlantic Monthly* in February 1998— "Can't Anyone Here Play This Game"—some senior CIA officials anonymously or off the record conceded that recruitment exaggeration and fraud had been a problem in the Directorate of Operations (a senior official from George Tenet's office came to see me and said so directly). They always added, of course, that things had changed. "George Tenet is really making the DO a much more effective organization" were the words of Tenet's messenger.[6]

6. It is important to note that Goss *is* making major changes in personnel overseas. According to active-duty CIA officers, the director has already removed several chiefs of station and other senior personnel abroad, causing one senior case officer to call this effort a "purge." The early "rotation" of personnel appears to be preceding one geographic division at a time, with all divisions scheduled for similar reviews. However, according to CIA case officers, this purge is not happening because of concerns over recruitment exaggeration and fraud or a desire to fundamentally change the DO personnel, management, and cover structure overseas. According to one officer, Goss is just "trying to shake things up" by recalling senior personnel from areas of insufficient operational activity. As most "big" stations and bases in Europe and East Asia divisions *really* don't see that much unilateral operational activity—even using the DO's loose understanding of what worthwhile operational activity is—such purges could potentially touch many officers. Removing one chief of station or base and replacing him or her with another case officer, raised in and loyal to the "old school," who will

But Tenet didn't do that, and neither is Porter Goss. Talk to active-duty case officers who are not vested in the system, and they'll quickly tell you that this institution-destroying problem is alive and well because the DO organizational structure overseas and its methods of operation are unchanged. My Cold War era description of how CIA stations routinely operated is, mutatis mutandis, applicable to different targets in the twenty-first century. The cover and structure of how officers are stationed remains the same: The majority of CIA officers overseas do not, 24/7, chase the Islamic terrorist target, and those who do usually do so using tried-and-true methods that operationally (and morally) bankrupted the agency during the Cold War. According to active-duty operatives, counterterrorist-focused case officers must still make their ends meet by playing the traditional espionage game, always hunting for the "target of opportunity," somebody they can describe to station management and headquarters as a worthwhile "developmental" or recruitment. As standards remain low in the CIA, this isn't particularly difficult: Tagging these recruitments as "access agents" to hard targets is a time-honored favorite inside the service. Legions of assets were so put on the books during the Cold War. According to CIA officials, case officers are now starting to do the same with foreigners who, in agency operational cables at least, have access to Islamic terrorist targets.

As in the past, operatives today cannot afford to focus exclusively on a difficult, elusive target, for fear of becoming noncompetitive with their colleagues who are not primarily working the counterterrorist beat. Counterterrorist-focused case officers overseas are, again, similar to Soviet–East Europe division case officers

work in overseas "inside-officer" stations and bases that, by their very nature, maintain the "DO culture," will accomplish little. It is likely that Goss's efforts will actually feed the directorate's constant hunger for easy recruitments, as new station and base chiefs, and the attentive foot soldiers below them, energetically try to create more work.

of yesteryear. They could not afford to work exclusively the SE target, either behind the Iron Curtain as denied-area officers servicing "dead-drops" and occasionally meetings agents or in the other area divisions trying to meet Soviet and East Europeans at cocktail parties, sporting events, and expatriate British pubs.

In other words, the Islamic terrorist target has become for the Clandestine Service what the Soviets were during the Cold War: the seldom met, let alone recruited, enemy who justifies a global service vastly too large for it to be honest and effective. The myth of recruiting Soviet and hard-core East European and Cuban targets sustained the institution's esprit de corps and made it easier for case officers to deceive themselves about their espionage profession.[7] The myth of recruiting counterterrorist agents against al Qaeda and other militant Islamic organizations is now developing. The success

---

7. For an amusing description of how the CIA has changed its focus to terrorism, see Lindsay Moran's commentary on CIA case officer training in *Blowing My Cover: My Life as a CIA Spy and Other Misadventures* (Putnam Adult, 2004). Confronting totalitarian security services is out at "the Farm," the agency's training facility in rural Virginia; terrorists are in. There is nothing in theory wrong with this. However, what is notable about Ms. Moran's junior-officer experience is the continuing mediocrity of the espionage training: the laughter-provoking badness of the spy instructors and the Farm's management. Al Qaeda has replaced the KGB; otherwise, *plus ça change, plus ça reste le même*. What good junior officers have discovered when they leave the Farm is that case officers at headquarters and overseas aren't necessarily better than the professional "failures" they had as instructors. The Farm is the first important step in the conditioning of officers to accept the operational surreality of the whole institution. Ms. Moran is also a good read about the frustration and uselessness that many case officers—the thoughtful ones—feel when they look at the mediocre foreign-intelligence agents they recruit and run. Ms. Moran was overwhelmed with this malaise post-9/11, given the pettiness of what she was doing and the urgency and seriousness of the threat against the United States (see, in particular, Moran, pp. 270–288). Feeling frustrated and useless has always been a common theme among educated case officers who take their jobs seriously. The sensation is dulled somewhat when case officers have fun in their work—when operatives, particularly male operatives, are enjoying themselves and occasionally feeling the adrenaline surge, they tend to believe that the work they're doing is serious and important to the nation.

of using counterterrorism to increase agency funding and staffing is already proven. The odds are very good that the agency will now see several more decades of intelligence malfeasance without serious reflection and internal reform. The 9/11 Commission utterly failed to take on the Directorate of Operations, as it also failed to dissect the operational problems of the Federal Bureau of Investigation. The Commission on the Intelligence Capabilities of the United States Regarding Weapons of Mass Destruction, which issued the so called Robb-Silberman Report (named after the cochairs, former Senator Charles Robb and former federal Judge Laurence Silberman) did a somewhat better job, recognizing systemic problems within the Directorate of Operations and making serious (though often inadequate) recommendations on how to improve the performance of the Clandestine Service.[8] However, the

---

8. Though the Robb-Silberman report is easily the most serious effort yet by Washington to review the intelligence collection performance of the Directorate of Operations, it still suffers, as did the 9/11 Commission's recommendations, from a top-down view of the CIA. The report is critical of traditional CIA clandestine intelligence collection techniques post-9/11 and understands that "new platforms for human intelligence" need to be strengthened (the sometimes awkward bureaucratic language of the report, I am told, abates in the classified version, where there is a more detailed discussion of the inadequacy and failures of "inside" case officers against specific targets and why, in particular, the nonofficial cover cadre needs to become more prominent in CIA operations). Yet the report fundamentally fails to grasp the capacity of the Directorate of Operations to corrupt the efficacy of its recommendations. The report envisions "Target Development Boards," "Innovation Centers," and operationally savvy "Mission Managers" all coming together to provide an "integrated . . . strategic management of [human] collection" for the entire intelligence community. With more centralized planning and management, all under the watchful eye of the new national intelligence director, operations will benefit from greater synergies—putting better talent on the right spot at the right time, and underscoring and correcting weaknesses more quickly.

To quote from the report: "The Target Development Board will then study all available collection capabilities from across the Community to the intelligence 'gaps' we have in our understanding of Country X's program. If collectors come up short in filling these "gaps," the Mission Manager may recommend more aggressive collection techniques involving higher risk strategies. Because it is a standing entity, the Target Development Board will be able to quickly revisit pri-

report's issuance was largely upstaged by the illness and death of Pope John Paul II: It did not, and is now not likely, to generate the attention and public pressure that such reports require to galvanize action against resistant, accomplished bureaucratic power players. (With the possible exception of the Pentagon, the CIA, which has always been dominated by the Directorate of Operations, is the most politically adept bureaucracy in Washington.) The publicity-devouring 9/11 Commission also had already sucked up most of the oxygen in the capital necessary to sustain a serious intelligence debate.

Congress and the White House are unlikely once more to work up the self-flagellatory energy to severely question Langley about its operational prowess unless we get hit again inside the United

---

orities in response to changing events, and adjust the collection strategy correspondingly." Sounds fine in theory. In reality, these new offices are going to be staffed by CIA case officers—or Pentagon case officers schooled by Langley (and Robb-Silverman wants to *increase* Langley's control of case officer education). Robb-Silverman somehow envisions these new entities as existing outside of the Directorate of Operations—the report, without exploring the origins of the DO's culture, understands that the culture is toxic—but within the CIA.

This is a meaningless bureaucratic division. Senior and midlevel case officers raised in the Clandestine Service's defective system will *immediately* take over Robb-Silberman's new CIA.

Langley has rarely not known what the truly important targets are supposed to be. A Target Development Board will just repeat the targets that the CIA knows it *ought* to hunt seriously. The CIA has always had "mission managers"—chiefs of station and base have always directed junior officers toward these targets (and other more reliable ones that guarantee case officer and station head counts). It would also be a demanding task to count up all the "innovative" operational cables DO management has sent out encouraging case officers to "think outside the box." Point: The headquarters, and especially overseas bureaucracy, makes the culture and the men and women of the Directorate of Operations. Until this bureaucracy is gutted—which means at first firing, not hiring, large numbers of case officers and radically rebuilding the way *most* case officers are deployed overseas—the many good ideas within the Robb-Silberman report have little chance of producing a more effective clandestine human intelligence collection program against America's hard-target enemies.

Given the influence and bureaucratic agility of the DO within the CIA, the Robb-Silberman report is much more likely to encourage the directorate's worst instincts and habits, not curtail them.

States on a 9/11 scale. Terrorist strikes outside the United States, on embassies, U.S. naval vessels, or American corporations, aren't likely to produce the heat necessary to change the status quo.

But Americans *are* Americans. If the CIA, or more likely outsiders with authority over Langley, ruthlessly conducted internal audits of recruitments and intelligence production, the system might possibly change by exposing the fictions—principally the recruitment myth—that have been used to support senior case officers and enable them to silence internal questioning and critics. Nobody really wanted to go there during the Cold War because both Republicans and Democrats had more or less accepted the agency's version of its own role in the battle against Communism. Even after the Cold War, a thoughtful, historically inclined, and intellectually curious CIA director like James Woolsey couldn't bring himself to severely probe CIA failings since he viewed the agency, and the Directorate of Operations in particular, as a national trust. This disposition is a natural one in Washington, especially among the elite of the foreign policy establishment. It combines well with a sense of self-preservation: What CIA or national intelligence director wants to publicly gut the organization that gives him pride of place among other senior officials? Who wants to go to work, knowing that he must fire hundreds of irremediably ineffective CIA employees to resuscitate the institution and endure savage press criticism for his actions? Confronted with policies they don't like, CIA officers will leak against CIA directors and presidents. Confronted with a director determined to transform Langley, they will leak nonstop to journalists always eager to find active-duty sources. (Those of us who have served in the Clandestine Service know well how seldom journalists actually have active-duty operational sources.)

The headlines are predictable: "New CIA Director Damages National Security" or "Novice CIA Chief Destroying Spy Networks Overseas" or, the worst, "Spy Professionals Defend CIA Against Neoconservative Director." And Langley always deploys a defense that an amazing number of journalists, congresspeople, executive-branch officials, and their staffers repeatedly fall for: "We've changed since these (disgruntled, embittered, noncompetitive) officers left the service." The Public Affairs office of the CIA and the authorized leakers from the "seventh floor" (the director's floor) shamelessly dump this line to the press. This routine is sometimes paired with controlled guided tours of CIA headquarters. A *Washington Post* journalist who had the intel beat once remarked to me that a senior case officer was walking him down Langley's hallways pointing to the cipher-locked doors. "If you only knew what great work was going on behind them," the CIA official volunteered. Frustrated and dependent upon the CIA for most of his access to Langley, the journalist wanted to be skeptical, but he didn't know how. Within a short period of time, his reporting disposition inclined him to give the Clandestine Service a *big* benefit of the doubt.

Inside the CIA, journalists who officially have the intelligence beat are rarely admired by good officers because the media usually give more weight to the official, "seventh-floor" line than they do to "dissident" commentary. (These journalists often fairly retort that working-level case officers won't talk to them, which is almost always true, so they inevitably become dependent on official leaks or retired senior case officers who are usually leaking on behalf of active-duty senior brethren.) Good and bad case officers are usually united in their distaste for the press. And the agency, particularly since 9/11, regularly hooks journalists who ought to know better with access to CIA paramilitary personnel. A look at the major newsmagazines after the beginning of the war in Afghanistan gives a good idea of how effective this tactic is. The discussion of pre-9/11 al Qaeda operations, or the lack thereof through most of the 1990s, receded. The sexiness of CIA paramilitary officers came to the foreground. The death of one paramilitary officer in a Taliban prison rebellion further shifted the limelight. The war in Iraq and the CIA's prewar assessments of Saddam Hussein's WMD programs moved the spotlight unfavorably, but the possibility remains omnipresent that a CIA paramilitary operation in Afghanistan or elsewhere could again change the barometer. CIA paramilitary actions have certainly had their successes—as have DO espionage operations—but they are fundamentally different from the routine counterterrorist and noncounterterrorist espionage work that occurs at headquarters and in CIA stations and bases abroad. This work—not the special ops—has always defined the agency and the so-called "DO culture."

In vain in the 1990s did former "dissident" ex–case officers suggest that American bureaucracy, particularly secret bureaucracy, was not magically exempt from Max Weber's rules and insights. Secret bureaucracies more stubbornly resist change than all others because they can more effectively insulate themselves. If that *Washington Post* journalist had been able to secrete himself behind the doors of Langley's Counterterrorism Center before 9/11, he would have seen that, contrary to what George Tenet was discreetly telling selected members of the press, Osama bin Ladin and al Qaeda had very little to fear from the Clandestine Service. If journalists today could get behind those same doors, they'd find methods, if not attitudes, little changed. The war in Afghanistan and the security-service dragnets put into place post-9/11 in many countries have done enormous damage to al Qaeda and other Islamic militant organizations with a jihadist edge. But this success owes *very* little to what case officers call "unilateral intelligence operations"—efforts by the DO, without any liaison with a foreign-security or intelligence organization, to develop sources within radical Islamic groups.

Add up all the factors against change at the CIA, and it ought to be clear that we are now stuck with a moribund Clandestine Service. Whatever revolutionary impetus existed post-9/11 has evaporated. President Bush's decision to retain the services of George Tenet, a want-to-be DO operative with exceptional political skill, and the utter failure of the 9/11 Commission to deconstruct the service and its decades-old problems ended the opportunity to radically alter the way Langley does its work. If the United States gets attacked again by Islamic holy warriors, it's possible, assuming the magnitude of the strike is horrific, that the reform of the Directorate of Operations might again become a topic of serious debate. Americans, at least Americans outside the government, are inclined toward change and well tolerate painful corporate restructuring. With the image of a nuclear mushroom cloud over New York City, Americans would surely embrace a good deal of creative destruction at Langley.

Let us suppose that a revolution in Virginia was possible without another 9/11. What would a more operationally effective clandestine service look like?

First and foremost, it would be much smaller and overwhelmingly weighted in favor of the nonofficial cover officer, always known in the trade as a NOC (pronounced "knock"). The CIA would still have stations and bases abroad located within official U.S. facilities, but their focus would no longer be on the recruitment of foreign agents. Even the biggest stations ought to have just a handful of officers: a station chief, who would primarily be a liaison officer with the host country's security and intelligence services and who would have absolutely no control over NOC operations in his or her country; a deputy, who also would be essentially a liaison officer; a nondeclared consular-covered case officer who never did liaison work would be necessary in posts where visas had a decent chance of offering avenues into radical Muslim or Middle Eastern communities; and a communications specialist and an administrative assistant to make up the rest of the typical station. The CIA would have to make a special case—and the bar should be *very* high—for nondeclared "unilateral case officers" working under official, nonconsular cover. There may well be compelling reasons for such operatives here and there, particularly on a temporary basis, but the congressional oversight committees and the White House should assume that Langley will try to bloat the size of its required workforce.

And it wouldn't be that hard to verify CIA requests. A critical review of past intelligence reporting from that post would quickly reveal whether "inside" fake-diplomat case officers had produced serious reporting from "developmentals," or sources recruited by operatives working under official cover. The congressional oversight committees and the White House could create a small standing organization of intelligence-report reviewers—an independent non-CIA inspector general for human intelligence collection. Assuming the reviewers had basic competency, they would rapidly see whether unilateral reporting from a given post had substantially added to our knowledge—that is, it did not mirror State Department reporting or offer commentary remarkably similar to that given in newspapers such as *al-Quds*, *al-Hayat*, *Sharq al-Awsat*, or the *New York Times*. (Competent reviewers on al Qaeda and Islamic extremism should have a background in the Middle East, some should be fluent in Arabic, and none should be detailed from the agency.) If Langley couldn't demonstrate a track record of high-quality reporting from "inside" officers, then further staffing at the stations in question should be rejected.

The objective here is to break the back of the bureaucracy that has maintained the Clandestine Service recruitment myth for nearly fifty years. If we do not destroy this employment and governing structure within the Directorate of Operations, then the service will not be able to heal itself and develop operations that have greater odds of penetrating Islamic terrorist networks. Even if the CIA, under pressure from the outside, were to form a special, unconventional operations unit devoted to Islamic extremism, the effort would be for naught because institutionally the DO would co-opt or smother it. The headquarters DO management, formed in the old, now parallel system, would still control it. Conventional personnel policies would still guide the ambitions of the case officers temporarily assigned to it. The overseas outposts of this unit would still be terminally hamstrung by "inside officer" culture, cover, and leadership. As bureaucratically and politically appealing as it might be to start small—to try to build a new Clandestine Service within the old one—mechanically, it just doesn't make sense.[9] The "old" Directorate of Operations will win. To improve our odds against Islamic holy warriors and to allow for smaller, more creative, intelligent counterterrorist units to form, a full frontal assault on the DO is required.

Shrinking the size of stations and bases is both the easiest and most essential reformatory first step. With this reduction in force, Congress and the White House would reduce the size of the DO by about a half. Such a reduction would, of course, be paired with a thorough review of case officer deployment at headquarters and domestic stations and bases, which also accounts for a fairly substantial amount of personnel. Stateside DO work entails many different functions. Historically, ethically sensitive types, who wanted to avoid the integrity-crushing recruitment imperative of the DO overseas, or real operational losers—alcoholics, sloppy womanizers, case officers guilty of truly gross negligence abroad, and the mentally challenged—usually provided the DO compliment for CIA outposts across the country, including the Farm. At home, like abroad, the CIA should prove to outsiders that staff officers actually contribute to the CIA's primary intelligence collection missions.[10]

9. This is essentially what the Robb-Silberman report is recommending through the creation of a Human Intelligence Directorate within the CIA but outside the Directorate of Operations. The objective of this new directorate would be "to serve as a national human intelligence authority, exercising the responsibility to ensure the coordination of all agencies conducting human intelligence operations on foreign soil."

10. Shutting down the Farm as *the* training facililty for nonparamilitary operatives would, by itself, make agency espionage training more serious. A real junior-officer program would exclusively use major cities—the more frustrating, the better—in the United States and abroad for all espionage training.

Again, this isn't that hard to do. In theory, Langley has had a
large number of officers, spanning several different offices, working
the Islamic terrorist target since September 10, 2001. According to
Tenet, the agency was working hard on this menace years before.
This work should be verified. Also, the intelligence production from
headquarters-based officers (since the end of the Cold War, the CIA
has been basing an increasing number of intelligence-collecting
operational officers in ever larger task forces, centers, and country
desks at Langley) should be reviewed. If the number of officers
grossly exceeds the valuable information produced—and according
to active-duty CIA officers, there is no connection whatsoever to the
number of officers working the al Qaeda beat and the clandestine
intelligence produced—then start firing case officers. A serious
review of personnel would quickly show that the clandestine service
is vastly overstaffed with "inside" operatives. The number of these
officers at headquarters and in stations and bases working against
the Islamic terrorist target is simply surreal given the poor utility
of these officers against this target. Truth be told—and active-duty
CIA officers who actually do have the right qualifications to work
the Middle Eastern beat are scathing in their critique of the current
DO cadre—the number of case officers with the right language and
educational skills to work the Islamic radical target are too few to
cover counterterrorism, let alone any other issues in the Middle
East (for example, Iraq). And the pruning of operatives working the
counterterrorist beat should be repeated for all priority targets.

Review the way the Clandestine Service has handled North
Korea, pre- and post-war Iraq, Iran, the Peoples Republic of China,
and other countries of somewhat less magnitude that are nevertheless critical to the generation of Islamic extremism, for example,
Egypt and Saudi Arabia. If the methods have not made sense—and
in most cases, outsiders will discover that the Directorate of Operations has been neither particularly creative nor successful in

approaching these targets—then responsible case officers should be superannuated.

Given how little case officer support is required to sustain overseas officially covered case officers—who cannot, in any case, usually chase, develop, and recruit anyone useful against the Islamic extremist target—the support and management structure the DO has developed is massive. What is truly striking about the operations directorate today is how bureaucratically top heavy it has become given the size of the Clandestine Service, which is, in total number, a relatively small corporation. The State Department, a much larger organization, has a *slightly* more advanced case of this bureaucratic malaise: Foreign service officers and the civil servants in the department spend vastly more time "feeding the beast"—the in-house, mercilessly vertical paper machine that is Foggy Bottom—than conveying information about foreigners. As the Clandestine Service continues its decades-old evolution toward becoming a barely covert version of Foggy Bottom, the paper-pushing headquarters hierarchy has become an excellent vehicle for rapid career advancement (where "scalp hunting" abroad was once the sine qua non for the ambitious). In particular, the impressive growth in the CIA of the case officer cadre dealing with foreign intelligence and security services in the past ten years has further diminished the early agency's frontier, antibureaucratic "cowboy" ethic, which was virtually dead before.

To put it simply, the "inside" highly bureaucratized DO culture has to be replaced with a personnel system geared overwhelmingly to nonofficial cover officers. Where today NOCs represent a *very* small slice of the DO force, in a Clandestine Service aimed first and foremost at the radical Islamic target, NOCs ought to represent at least one third to one half of the directorate. They should be the overwhelming majority of all "unilateral" case officers. Remember: We don't need an army of nonofficial cover officers. During the Casey years, the CIA hired too many NOCs and deployed them overseas with often astoundingly bad business cover that usually didn't have much to do with targets chased. Senior "inside" case officers outside the Soviet–East Europe division have rarely ever cared much about cover—it gets in the way of "scalp hunting"—and they have dominated the operations directorate since its founding. This mentality bled over into the subordinate NOC force, where its senior officers, like their "inside officer" counterparts, usually attained their higher ranks by playing fast and loose with recruitments. When the CIA tries to deploy a nonofficial cover operative into an extremely dangerous environment, where the officer has an excellent chance of being killed or imprisoned for life if caught, using a cover legend of being a Band-Aid bandage salesman (and the agency hadn't even done a market survey to see whether imported Western Band-Aids were needed), you know your dealing with a mentally exhausted organization. Most NOCs currently serving are unquestionably unqualified to serve in the CIA. As mediocre as "inside officers" have usually been, NOCs have been worse. Virtually the entire NOC force should either be retired or fired.

The Clandestine Service needs a small, highly focused NOC cadre aimed at targets where it can make a difference. Against the jihadist target, nonofficial cover officers are really the only vehicle for penetrating Muslim radical organizations. Unlike "inside" officers, they can set up Muslim front organizations—charitable or educational societies aimed at attracting the kind of Muslim fundamentalists who have joined violent militant groups. They can much more naturally find prospective Muslim agents, who might possibly get close to, or join, radical Islamic associations that feed holy warrior organizations. Unlike "inside" officers, they can conceivably directly approach radical groups as prospective Muslim recruits. NOCs can come at these organizations from several different angles: as Muslim Arab-Americans, as John Walker Lindh white converts, as Black American–born or converted Muslims, as Joseph Padilla–type Hispanic converts, or as third-country (French, English, Mexican, Canadian, African, or Chinese) Muslims angry at the United States. Properly chosen and properly trained, nonofficial cover officers can hit these organizations worldwide. The mission will certainly be dangerous, which will be part of the appeal to the young men and women who would join this new NOC force. If they stay alive, case officers in this work cannot expect to last long. The option for nonofficial officers to retire with a full pension as early as forty would not be unreasonable. The world of Islamic militants is unavoidably a young person's domain. Starting salaries for such operatives should be in the six figures—a beginning salary of $250,000 would be appropriate given the high risks involved and the difficulty the CIA will have attracting and keeping Americans with the right qualifications. The agency is an "exempted service" precisely because national security is not an area where civil service regulations should apply. Egalitarianism—the public service sentiment that says case officers should not make more than diplomats, soldiers, or U.S. senators—has no place in an organization trying to penetrate groups that want to nuke the United States.

Again, the CIA will need all the help it can get to attract the right kind of young men and women. Admission standards must be demanding. For example, the British Indian Civil Service required successful applicants to have first, and occasionally second, degree university awards in the hardest subjects. It did not like, for example, to take honors students from Middle Eastern language programs because it did not consider a first in Arabic to be as reliably rigorous as a first in Ancient Greek. Anyone who conquered the classics was assumed to be capable of mastering Persian, the administrative language of both the Indian Moguls and the British. English pedantry aside, this type of elitism—at all times mixed with an American appreciation for practical experience and an un-American appreciation for youthful lives spent abroad—couldn't hurt the CIA. But it won't save it. Only destroying the bureaucracy and operational ethics of "inside" case officers can salvage the place. But higher admissions standards would go a long way to building a meaningful esprit de corps in the all-critical early years of a case officer's life.[11]

Setting high standards for everyone is key. The CIA's mission is to penetrate radical Islamic groups. The White House and Congress ought to set demanding objectives and then hold case officers, particularly senior case officers, to them.[12] There is a wide variety of Islamic fundamentalist organizations. Some are more aggressively ecumenical than others. Some are dangerous. Some aren't. Many, if not most, may offer some valuable information in America's battle against holy warrior Islam. Give the CIA's counterterrorism units a sliding time scale for penetrating these organizations (not much time would be required to get inside the Pakistani-headquartered Tablighat; years might be required to secrete someone into the al Qaeda-allied, Europe-based *Groupe Salafiste pour la Prédication et le Combat*). Regularly review the agency's work and start firing case officers who fail to advance the mission. Good case officers may occasionally get unfairly punished, but the odds are excellent that worthless operatives will be removed from service in much greater numbers. If we are in a war, we should have wartime

11. Higher admission standards won't overcome the in-house security inquisitors, polygraphs in hand, who often, through the best of intentions, stand guard against the CIA, attracting an ethnically mixed, religiously diverse, well-traveled junior officer cadre. The fiasco of Aldrich Ames, a white-bread American mole for the Soviets, supercharged Langley's counterintelligence sensibilities. A parochial admissions system got worse. The idea of preemptive counterespionage—weeding out potential trouble as early as possible—took over the institution. Counterintelligence branches of intelligence services are rarely staffed with men and women of cosmopolitan background. Too much deviation from certain accepted American norms can make your chances of getting into the CIA exiguous. If left unchecked by agency management, or outsiders who have the authority to interfere, counterintelligence officers can easily become too zealous for the institution's own well-being.

12. The Robb-Silberman report should be complimented for trying to go in this direction. Concerning standards and the Directorate of Operations, the 9/11 Commission is mute.

standards for achievement. From 1941 to 1944, the U.S. Army demoted and spit out an enormous number of incompetent officers. From September 11, 2001, to today, how many CIA operatives have been fired for failure to penetrate radical Islamic organizations? The odds are that the answer is "zero."

What must be avoided at all costs is President Bush's planned 50 percent increase in the size of the Clandestine Service. There are very few good recommendations to come out of the 9/11 Commission, and hiring more case officers was one of the worst. And the Robb-Silberman report goes even further in recommending the "bigger is better" ethic for American espionage.[13] If one reviews the CIA's operational messes over the past forty years, the Casey years would probably win as the period of the most damning *espionage* failures. Casey didn't directly have anything to do with the awful performance of American intelligence, particularly counterintelligence, during his tenure. But there is a very good argument to make that Casey's and President Reagan's decision to flood the CIA with cash and new personnel—when I entered in 1985, old-timers regularly referred to the Casey years as "a new golden age," the best since the 1950s—accelerated Langley's rot by massively expanding

13. Inside the classified Robb-Silberman report, this commission offers "statistics showing how badly outgunned our human intelligence collectors are, at precisely the time when the most is expected of them. Although we make few recommendations that we believe will require substantial budget increases, we do believe that this is an area where increased funding for the purpose of expanding human intelligence forces would be appropriate." Now, it would be inappropriate for me to enumerate exactly what are the personnel resources of the Directorate of Operations, but its total number of case officers is, assuming the cadre were qualified for its primary missions and deployed intelligently overseas, surely too large, not too small, for the tasks at hand. As the operations directorate had vastly too many people "officially" allocated to Soviet–East European targets during the Cold War, it has too many operatives now aimed at the terrorist target. Espionage is not a military operation: The odds of success don't improve with bulk. If this weren't true, the CIA would have done a *vastly* better job against a wide variety of Cold War and Middle Eastern targets.

the case officer cadre and, with it, recruitment and intelligence-reporting exaggeration and fraud.

This hunger for recruitments reached its ugliest crescendo in the great Iranian takedown of 1988 to 1989 and in the Cuban doubles fiasco, where Cuban intelligence successfully dangled and turned probably every single CIA asset in Cuba. The Cuban fiasco stretched over at least two decades, but there is good reason to believe that the successes of Cuban intelligence increased significantly in the 1980s when CIA case officers, especially those from the Latin America division, became ever-more greedy in their quest to recruit Cubans and get promoted.[14] The Iranian roll-up, which was probably the most lethal mess the CIA had experienced since the covert-action nightmares of the early Cold War in Eastern Europe and China, and the Cuban counterespionage coup were the unintended by-products of Casey's commendable desire to improve America's intelligence capabilities. Porter Goss and George W. Bush will inevitably add fat to the same fire unless they first overturn the rule and bureaucracy of "inside" case officers. America's war on Islamic militancy was a godsend to America's secret bureaucrats. The Cold War gave them a sustaining myth for forty years. For a decade, they lived without a replacement. The war on terror has now given them another, and rest assured they will run with it. It's a very good thing for the United States that we are likely to win this war, as we won the last one, because of American might and the global appeal of democracy. If we had to depend on the CIA, Islamic radicals and rogue states would have *much* better odds.

---

14. See on CIA being duped by Cuba and East Germany, Michael Wines and Ronald J. Ostrow, "Cuban Defector Claims Double Agents Duped U.S." *Washington Post*, August 12, 1987, A8. According to the former ranking minority member of the House Permanent Select Committee on Intelligence, "almost all" recruited "East German 'agents'" were found to be 'doubles'" as well (Bud Shuster, "HiTech vs. Human Spying," *Washington Times*, February 11, 1992, F3).

5

The Role of Science and Technology in Transforming American Intelligence

Kevin M. O'Connell

I. OVERVIEW

Among the most important legacies of modern-day American intelligence is its emphasis on science and technology. Technical programs such as the U2 reconnaissance aircraft and the CORONA photo reconnaissance satellite provided independent perspectives for corroborating, modifying, or adding to the information provided by spies operating against the Soviet Union and its allies. The early success of these and other programs in signals intelligence (SIGINT), imagery intelligence (IMINT), and measurement and signature intelligence (MASINT) created an impetus for technical intelligence that was unmatched by any other kind of intelligence capabilities during the Cold War.[1] Beyond an improved understanding of the Soviet Union as a political and ideological enemy, technical intelli-

---

1. See Loch Johnson, *Secret Agencies: U.S. Intelligence in a Hostile World* (New Haven, CT: Yale University Press, 1996), 14–26.

gence collection capabilities and the use of technology to support analysis, counterintelligence, and covert action provided a unique intelligence advantage over our adversaries.

Yet if science and technology represent a major component of the American intelligence enterprise, they have thus far received little attention within major reviews and legislative initiatives. Neither the Intelligence Reform and Terrorism Prevention Act of 2004 (hereafter, the Intelligence Reform Act) nor *The 9/11 Commission Report* devoted much time and attention to science and technology and their roles in U.S. intelligence. This is somewhat surprising. To be sure, recent headlines have dampened appreciation of the value of technical intelligence programs and, in part, focused attention in other areas, particularly the perceived failures in the cases of the 9/11 terrorist attacks on the homeland and Iraqi weapons of mass destruction (WMD) programs. At the same time, the increasing complexity and high costs of technical programs, as well as the continuing concerns about the ability to manage science and technology programs, have raised legitimate questions about whether they can and how they should remain a key element of American intelligence. Yet today's intelligence struggles in the global war on terrorism (GWOT) against proliferators of WMD and other illicit goods, and even in regard to advanced conventional threats demand technical intelligence insights. And there are high expectations for science and technology in helping to solve some of the more modern aspects of intelligence, like the analyst's challenge of information overload and the visualization of complex phenomena like radar and biological data.[2]

2. As of this writing, but too late for full inclusion in this chapter, the final report of the Commission on Intelligence Capabilities of the United States Regarding Weapons of Mass Destruction was released. It is sharply and deeply critical of U.S. intelligence performance on Iraq's WMD programs, indcluding numerous challenges to U.S. technical collection in the chemical, biological, and nuclear arenas. The report discusses many of the primary and underlying issues raised in this chapter and strongly recommends an emphasis on creating a more inte-

Aside from what technical intelligence programs can do is the issue of how to undertake them. Historically, what made them successful were an unwavering focus on the conceptualization and development of new capabilities, an emphasis on risk-taking, dedicated and flexible investment, and the nurturing of human capital or people with critical technical talent. Well beyond today's headlines lie these critical management challenges.

This chapter begins with a discussion of technology's impact on intelligence in the early part of the twenty-first century. It then turns to a discussion of how technology contributes to various intelligence disciplines and identifies some of the key technologies that may be useful to intelligence functions during the coming years. It contains a lengthy discussion about how to stimulate, nurture, and manage the development of technical capabilities for intelligence, which require a reorientation both on internal management processes and on external linkages. Development raises basic questions of focus, risk, investment, and people, as well as some higher level issues related to the link between requirements and capabilities, internal management processes, and challenges to the industrial base. The chapter then concludes with observations on how science and technology can contribute to the transformation of U.S. intelligence.

---

grated collection enterprise—including target development, investment, and system development—and the strong need to reinvigorate innovation across the intelligence community. The panel also envisioned roles for science and technology as key enablers for better analysis, collaboration, information sharing, and other essential intelligence functions. Any reader interested in this topic will also make use of the commissions report at www.wmd.gov.

II. THE CHANGING TECHNOLOGY ENVIRONMENT FOR INTELLIGENCE

Technology and the Era of Transparency

Today, various technologies create the means for governments, intelligence services, and even individuals to gather and interpret information about others that was historically held only in the coffers of intelligence services in Washington and Moscow. Because of the information and communications revolution, access to this information is often exceptionally fast and relatively inexpensive. The era of transparency is upon us.

At the same time, the world of terrorist cells and the illicit trade in, among other items, weapons of mass destruction that intelligence targets remains murky. Accordingly, transparency does not mean that everything is completely open, nor that it should be. It means rather that there are increasingly unprecedented types and amounts of information available to any one interested party about almost any other.[3]

More precisely, while American intelligence has a wealth of both classified and unclassified information sources from which to draw, so to do our adversaries.[4] Much of the electronic data that al Qaeda acquired prior to the 9/11 attacks, for example, came from Web sites, later verified by individuals performing their own surveillance. Beyond Internet-based sources of analysis about foreign military and security developments, new technical sources of information—such as global positioning system (GPS) navigational data, commercial space imagery, and biometrics—are also available to

3. For a generalized discussion about transparency, see David Brin, *The Transparent Society: Will Technology Force Us to Choose Between Privacy and Freedom?* (Reading, MA: Addison Wesley, 1998). For a more specific reference to intelligence, see John Baker, et al., *Commercial Observation Satellites: At the Leading Edge of Global Transparency* (Bethesda, MD: RAND-ASPRS, 2001).

4. See Kevin O'Connell and Robert Tomes, "Keeping the Information Edge," *Policy Review* 122 (2004): 19–39.

anyone who has an interest and a modest budget. Coupled with instantaneous communication through cell phones, instant messaging, e-mail, and other sources, foreign governments and nongovernmental actors can be part of a "virtual" surveillance team, military action group, or terrorist cell.

While some might believe that intelligence is immune to such developments, it is actually in many ways driven by transparency. The first aspect of the issue, driven as much by spy novels, media leaks, and counterintelligence disasters as it is by technology, is that the traditional tools of espionage are now well known in detail, thereby diminishing some of their value. Even the simplest-minded adversary knows that intelligence services use both human and technical means to conduct intelligence, including the collection of telephone calls and other signals, the taking of pictures and other images from space, and the use of sophisticated technical sensors to look for specialized signs of harm. They also know, of course, that the embassy cocktail circuit no longer serves as a purely innocent venue within which to share information, unless one is looking to be recruited. For an even more sophisticated adversary, additional information is known, such as the methods of agent debriefing, the susceptibility of technical intelligence to deception, and the predictability of satellite orbits.[5]

But transparency's implications for intelligence range much farther, creating, in essence, a "loss of exclusivity" for most intelligence tools and techniques. Beyond the realm of sophisticated technical intelligence systems, an entire slate of commercial technologies has both explicit and implicit utility as a tool of surveillance and intelligence. Modern cities are replete with video surveillance, for example, and the prevalence of GPS embedded in navigational and other technologies is designed to help one find out where he

---

5. See Dennis Gormely, "The Limits of Intelligence: Iraq's Lessons," *Survival: The IISS Quarterly* 46, no. 3 (2004): 7–29.

or she is (thereby potentially helping others as well): The salesman pitching a father purchasing a cell phone for his daughter assures the father how good he will feel knowing that the phone's location can be determined, whether after curfew or under more serious conditions. Other modern conveniences, such as credit cards, Internet portal access, electronic toll paying, electronic car safety, and security systems not only help pinpoint people's location but also identify many of their habits.

Although strong concerns certainly exist within the American public about the intelligence community's access to and use of these data, they are clearly of potential value as intelligence sources. The Defense Advanced Research Projects Agency's Total Information Awareness (later Terrorism Information Awareness) program, for example, was envisioned as arraying these and other data sets in the hopes of identifying anomalies and improving efficiency in the use of existing intelligence information about suspected terrorists. But if American intelligence might tap these sources, so might others, and almost certainly under fewer restrictions. Aside from the broader social and economic implications of this data-gathering by others—witness, for example, the rapid rise in identity theft—technologies like biometrics and tracking tools represent challenges to human intelligence (HUMINT) and covert action.

In other words, the information age may have spawned a new intelligence age, an age that might be characterized as a footrace between intelligence services, including a constant race for U.S. intelligence to provide information to national security decision makers better than our adversaries can. In these circumstances, the United States is running a series of footraces against multiple adversaries simultaneously, including nation-states as well as terrorists, all focused on defeating American intelligence activities in the context of their own strategies and security activities.[6]

6. O'Connell and Tomes, "Keeping the Information Edge."

Clearly, transparency holds both promise and threat for U.S. intelligence, with important implications for the roles of science and technology. If transparency is the norm, sanctuaries and hiding places will become highly valued by our adversaries. Intelligence will be operating in a much less structured framework and against a much more organizationally and technically complex target set, which will limit the ability of agencies to organize around a predictable set of security issues that have specific collection targets. Flexibility and adaptation are key. The pursuit of an "information edge" will have to take place within a context of a more diffuse and dynamic global information technology environment and an increased ability by adversaries to collect information, protect information, and deceive U.S. intelligence agencies about their information and ours. This will place a premium on applying science and technology to developing unique intelligence capabilities across all intelligence functions and disciplines. If done correctly, the combination of persistent and exquisite technical intelligence capabilities and the reality of transparency will mean that sanctuary for our adversaries will come only at a premium, if not unaffordable, cost. Science and technology must be a key element of intelligence transformation.

III. THE CONTRIBUTIONS OF SCIENCE AND TECHNOLOGY TO U.S. INTELLIGENCE

From the early U2 spy plane and CORONA satellite to today's unmanned aerial vehicle (UAV) and SIGINT developments to tomorrow's future imagery architecture and space-based radar, U.S. intelligence draws, and will continue to draw, considerable insight from an extraordinary array of technical collection, processing, and exploitation capabilities. Science and technology make vital contributions to the classic areas of intelligence: collection, analysis, counterintelligence, and covert action. At the same time, the pace at which new technologies are emerging, their variety, and the threat they pose are creating additional challenges for U.S. intelligence.

When assessing the roles of science and technology, it is important to note that U.S. intelligence has drawn predominantly on technology and left the pure science to others. But as the overall and technical complexity of intelligence problems increases, basic scientific research, development, and expertise are playing increasingly important roles in sensing and exploiting complex technical intelligence data, such as those related to biological and chemical weapons or the penetrability of underground facilities.

Areas of Technological Focus

While technology supports all aspects of intelligence, it dominates the collection function through its role in SIGINT, IMINT, MASINT, and even the more recent construct of geospatial intelligence, or GEOINT,[7] which is the exploitation and analysis of imagery and geospatial information to describe, assess, and visually depict geographically referenced physical features and activities on Earth in support of national security information needs.[8] These capabilities are sometimes described collectively as technical intelligence sources, or TECHINT. From the exploitation of the electromagnetic spectrum to sensing and identifying unique elements (such as radionucleides), phenomena (such as terrain data), and signatures (such as temperatures or reflectants of certain metals or gases), technical collection helps create important raw inputs to U.S. intelligence. Beyond the pure sensing function, the combination of sensor technology and platform development—satellites, aircraft, and

7. See National Geospatial-Intelligence Agency (NGA). *National System for Geospatial Intelligence Statement of Strategic Intent: The Functional Manager's Perspective* (April 2004).
    8. Ibid., 3.

UAV—allows creative combinations for effective collection about our adversaries.

But technology's reach extends beyond collection. Technology also assists in conducting intelligence analysis by helping analysts sort, manage, highlight, and share data. Modern computing and communications capabilities allow for the use of complex models— such as exploratory modeling[9] and social network analysis—to understand multilayered relationships among people, events, and technologies. Within the realm of intelligence sharing, technology provides the foundation for expanded collaboration among analysts from diverse disciplines, agencies, and geographic locations, usually focused on a specific problem, like the activities of a terrorist cell or the status of the North Korean nuclear program. Data storage, communications, collaboration tools, and data mining technologies are of particular importance.

Although we might think of the gathering of all relevant information—usually in the head of a CIA or DIA all-source analyst—as fusion, technology today creates an opportunity for an even deeper horizontal integration of all available information. Sometimes referred to as a "multi-INT" analytic approach, horizontal integration is based on a set of capabilities designed to acquire, synchronize, correlate, and disseminate intelligence across sources and missions.[10] Some of the most operationally relevant intelligence during Operations Enduring Freedom and Iraqi Freedom was created in this fashion.

But there are substantial challenges as well. While technology's contributions to collection and analysis are evident, its contribution to the overall effectiveness of U.S. intelligence is less certain: Ques-

9. For one discussion about the use of models in intelligence, see Robert Clark, *Intelligence Analysis: A Target-Centric Approach* (Washington, DC: CQ Press, 2003), ch. 3–7.

10. National Geospatial-Intelligence Agency, *Horizontal Integration: Connecting the Unconnected* (2004).

tions range from the severe imbalance in using technology to collect data rather than to make use of it[11] to a debate that centers on whether technology can be a true source of sophisticated analysis or only an enabler—and perhaps a very good one—of human judgment. Although computers can generate, at lightning speed, many more hypotheses or potential outcomes from a data set than an analyst can—as in a game of computer chess—there remains no substitute for human judgment when trying to assess human behavior. Technology's real value today lies in increasing efficiency in both intelligence collection and analysis.

Technology also supports the counterintelligence and covert action functions, although in different ways. In the former case, technology's utility largely contributes to those same functions it provides to analysis, although new technologies are emerging to supplant the polygraph as the main tool by which to detect deception, whether by employee or by foreign agent.[12] In the case of covert action, technology potentially supports a set of capabilities that range from disguise and counterbiometric capabilities to tools for conducting influence operations, whether of a traditional nature or in cyberspace.

Emerging Technologies of Potential Importance

A diverse slate of technologies, if properly nurtured and managed with a view toward intelligence, has great potential to sustain the intelligence edge that America needs to stay ahead of its adversaries. Emerging space and sensor technologies will help intelligence move beyond the realm of black-and-white photography from

---

11. See Margaret MacDonald and Anthony Oettinger, "Information Overload: Managing Intelligence Technologies," *Harvard International Review*, Fall 2002: 44–48.

12. Various articles discuss new pathways in the neurosciences to detect political preferences, shopping preferences, and deception.

space. Other technologies will facilitate the collection of more advanced adversary telephone calls and radio and Web communications, while defending against similar threats that arise from them. Yet others will help spot a terrorist covertly at a long distance, while determining that the package he holds contains either food or fissile material. And yet others will mean less need for the risky, indeed potentially fatal, physical meetings that take place between case officer and agent. Elsewhere, computing and collaboration technologies will greatly expand the intellectual reach of the analyst to collector, colleague analyst, or even an outsider, in order to improve understanding of the content or context of a particular piece of information. And analysts' considerations of alternatives and complex situations will be enhanced by modeling, simulation, and visualization tools.

The new technologies are many and varied. Among them, advanced remote sensing, long-range photography, nanotechnology, quantum computing, biometrics, data mining, collaboration tools and devices, visualization, multilevel security, deception detection, and stealth merit attention for the collection and analysis of information about an adversary. And collection technologies will clearly benefit from increasingly adaptive platforms upon which to base them, whether under water, in the air, on the ground, or in the deep reaches of space. Analytic technologies will help with the organization and interpretation of data, the creation and testing of alternate hypotheses, and collaboration and visualization, both among analysts and between analysts and the policy makers they serve. And, as will be discussed, the quantum leaps taking place in the commercial world can only improve the chances of being faster, if not more sophisticated, in what intelligence is trying to understand and convey.

Technology Challenges

The unique role of technology in American intelligence carries its own imbalances and weaknesses, creating a potential vulnerability in the overall intelligence architecture, and therefore in our ability to understand our adversary's motives and intentions. Our use of technology to enhance our own intelligence performance carries a number of important challenges, each of which demands prompt attention.

The first challenge is that U.S. intelligence has been and remains overwhelmingly collection-centric, with insufficient attention paid to the creation of end-to-end (or sensor-to-analyst) architectures that will be needed to create useful and actionable intelligence. While technology can help make greater use of collected data, it must do so with relevant operational concepts and what might be called "metadata." For example, though constructing a massive database with current and archival data of all types may provide a powerful tool for an intelligence analyst, it will be useless without some regard for the education level, experience, and technical skill of the analyst who is using that database. Further, if horizontal integration is the wave of the future, it must accommodate more than a massive accumulation of data in the hope that "smoke, light, and heat"—one analyst's description of a fully comprehensive intelligence picture—will emerge. If data are not thought about more holistically—including how it can be processed, evaluated, and understood by both analysts and decision makers—utter confusion may just as likely be the outcome. Among other issues, consideration must be given to the relative values of specific pieces of information, their real or potential error values, and their overall potential utility in providing an intelligence assessment to someone with little or no experience in the exotica of intelligence.

The second challenge is that, as intelligence problems are becoming more complex, so are the means to understanding them.

In other words, current intelligence problems are not only organizationally more complex—increasingly transnational—but technically more complex as well. Technology's contribution here will be to develop both sophisticated algorithms and the visualization tools necessary to support the intelligence analyst and the decision makers that analysts are supporting. For example, we are moving well beyond the notion of satellite imagery intelligence as the analysis of mere pictures, as the science of remote sensing already extends into subpixel and molecular-level detail. At a minimum, the technical and economic trade-offs associated with turning these data back into pictures for intelligence are likely to be extraordinary. Further, the data collected by advanced remote sensing capabilities—such as multi- or hyperspectral data—are so rich and complex that they will require analysts to have or call upon those who possess technical skills in biology, chemistry, physics, and other disciplines that are uncommon within the ranks of U.S. intelligence yet vitally important to understanding phenomena related to weapons of mass destruction or other technical targets. And these data clearly force choices and trade-offs in collection, processing, and storage. Rather than a pure technology solution, some combination of organizational, technology, and other solutions will be necessary to ensure good analysis and actionable intelligence.

In other words, the complexity that the analyst faces must also be dealt with in presenting the intelligence analysis to decision makers. If a picture is worth a thousand words—especially for presidents, diplomats, and others who might try to persuade or compel others with pictures—then the direction of advanced remote sensing and the way it is used by decision makers run in opposite directions. Data will have to be turned back into pictures for such policy purposes. Similarly, for the decision maker who wishes to use an intercept for the same purposes—such as former Secretary of State Colin Powell at the United Nations in the run-up to the war with Iraq—the best and most sophisticated SIGINT will have little to do with the sound of a hushed voice whispering about his weapons program or operational plan. It will be much more the product of a technical signature, stripped out of a crush of signal noise and decrypted and processed through some of the most complex algorithms in the world. Although technology depends on an extremely complex set of processes, ultimately, its contribution is to simplify how the world is portrayed.

The third challenge, as the case of Iraq shows, is that technical intelligence often provides information that, in the face of an overall poor understanding of an issue or problem, has high potential to be misunderstood or misinterpreted.[13] Although most of the technical data released by the Bush administration, while sketchy, did point to elements of Iraqi WMD programs, these were misinterpreted in the context of an Iraqi regime that was either patently deceptive or whose servants found good cause to convince its leadership of these programs where there were little or none. Moreover, the success of U.S. technical intelligence over time has placed a premium on the denial and disguise of those capabilities by our adversaries, with everything from traditional camouflage to the rapid development of underground facilities in places like North Korea. As technical intelligence capabilities become more sophisticated, the vulnerability of both the collection and the analytic algorithms to deception will rise dramatically. Intelligence managers, technologists, and analysts must work hard to understand the technical phenomena related to proliferation, WMD, terrorism, and other technical problems.

The fourth challenge is that as new intelligence technologies are developed, managers must deal with intelligence and operational realities that will force them to innovate much faster than in the past. While American technical successes historically remained secret, at least to most of the world, tomorrow's intelligence tech-

13. See Gormely, "The Limits of Intelligence."

nologies will be drawn from a scientific and technical milieu that is accessible to the entire world.[14] Although countries or groups may not have the financial wherewithal to invest in these technologies for intelligence purposes, they may very well have the ability to understand and counter them, if not pursue limited capabilities that meet their own needs and purposes. In other words, while American intelligence can take advantage of advanced technologies, it will be difficult to keep sufficiently far ahead, given the pace at which the rest of the world is adopting new technology.[15] Aside from the natural proliferation of scientific knowledge in many areas, the commercialization of many technologies is advancing the spread of information relevant to both new threats and intelligence countermeasures.

An example might help. While America's SIGINT function took great advantage of the architectural stability and predictability of global communications in the 1970s, it has, for the past decade, struggled to keep up with the explosive rate of change in communications technologies and methods. There is not only an exponentially greater volume in communications, but also a much greater diversity in the types and methods used to secure them. Similar conditions are emerging in the GEOINT arena, as commercial sources of imagery and mapping data proliferate in the context of a rapidly changing environment for geographic information systems (such as maps and georectified data bases). Post-9/11 imperatives to share data will exacerbate this problem. Yet there is no going back. No classification system can stop the advance of science, nor should it. This places a premium on innovation in intelligence technologies.

14. This will vary across technical disciplines, of course. Numerous countries have advanced SIGINT capabilities, based on its traditional use in foreign intelligence systems. Even in the more modern case of imagery, countries are developing and accessing capabilities, combined with commercial geographic information system and other processes.

15. Taken from O'Connell and Tomes, "Keeping the Information Edge."

In this regard, the set of issues related to intelligence sharing and collaboration that, while by no means new for intelligence, has moved to the forefront since 9/11, especially in the homeland security arena, presents distinct challenges. Historically, access to technically sophisticated sources of intelligence was tightly controlled and handled on a need-to-know basis. A premium was placed on protecting intelligence sources and methods. Yet, as the 9/11 Commission and other reports indicate, the need-to-know principle is today turned on its head: In a world of terrorist threats, one may not know who needs to know, so it is imperative for U.S. intelligence to share with, say, coalition partners, law enforcement officers, or Coast Guard captains. While there are important counterintelligence dimensions of this new reality, its most important impact may be in the extreme pressures that it will create for the rapid development of new intelligence sources and methods.

In sum, technology has been, and remains, the darling of American intelligence, yet it presents both tremendous opportunity and risk. We will have to be both sophisticated and flexible in how we use technology and recognize that intelligence technology for its own sake is useless; only technology that gets unique information to the eyes, ears, and brains of America's intelligence analysts, both individually and collectively, has the promise of keeping us steps ahead of our adversaries. Understanding and selecting the technologies that will provide an intelligence advantage is hard enough. Providing the right context for developing them, knowing how to acquire them, and engineering their interaction with the intelligence community's most valuable resource—people—are equally difficult and certainly pose a very tough management task. We turn to this in the next section.

IV. MANAGING SCIENCE AND TECHNOLOGY RESOURCES FOR INTELLIGENCE

As mentioned, neither the Intelligence Reform Act nor the 9/11 Commission devoted much attention to science and technology matters. In fact, right beneath today's broad discussions about U.S. intelligence is an urgent, vitriolic, and sometimes melancholy debate about how to manage technical intelligence resources. A variety of management issues arises in connection to the creation of technical intelligence capabilities and the organizational foundations upon which they rely.

While the creation of a Director of National Intelligence and other initiatives has clear implications for the management of technical intelligence discussions and decisions, in places like the National Geospatial Intelligence Agency (NGA), National Security Agency (NSA), and National Reconnaisance Office (NRO) other discussions are much more focused on how to manage and advance these capabilities. These discussions must take into account the high cost and complexity of technical systems, a highly diverse set of intelligence requirements set forth by various U.S. national security constituencies (such as the Department of Defense, the CIA, and the Department of Homeland Security), and common government budgetary and acquisition practices. For example, officials conducted a relatively public comparison between the ability of former and current officials of the National Reconnaissance Office to acquire innovative satellite systems within cost, performance, and organizational constraints.[16] Other reports focus on the lack of management data with which intelligence community leaders can make effective trade-offs between intelligence capabilities, such as

16. See Robert Kohler, "One Officer's Perspective: The Decline of the National Reconnaissance Office," *Studies in Intelligence*. Followed by Dennis Fitzgerald, "Commentary on 'The Decline of the National Reconnaissance Office,'" *Studies in Intelligence* (2003).

space platforms and UAVs.[17] The failure to effectively set requirements or leverage the industrial base is the subject of yet other critiques and reports.[18] Technical intelligence capabilities can help maintain a comparative advantage over our adversaries only when they are effectively conceived, created, and managed.

The challenge is daunting, not only because of the difficulty of planning individual technical systems, but also because of the volume and diversity of requirements that have to be satisfied. Speed, collaboration, and creative analysis will be the key defining elements of the war on terror, while precision and persistence will dominate strategic and military intelligence requirements. Important trade-offs will have to be made between precise capability and the need for overall flexibility in a rapidly changing world. Similarly, decisions makers will have to weigh the use of new commercial capabilities—especially information technology—against government-designed systems, and consider trade-offs between near-term capabilities and experimentation for the future.

Today's U.S. intelligence community already has a wide range of centers and organizational subelements, such as the Intelligence Technology Innovation Center (ITIC) and Advanced Research and Development Agency (ARDA), CIA's Directorate of Science and Technology, the NRO's Advanced Systems and Technology Office, NGA's Innovision, and other organizations that emphasize technical solutions and forward-looking innovation. Other U.S. government agencies have broader departmental responsibilities, such as the Defense Advanced Research and Development Agency (DARPA) and the Science and Technology Directorate of the Department of Homeland Security (DHS). Although these offices have opportunities for considerable experimentation and outreach, they are also

17. See Richard Best, *Intelligence, Surveillance, and Reconnaissance Programs: Issues for Congress*, CRS Report for Congress, August 2004 (updated).
18. See Baker et al., *Commercial Observation Satellites*.

plagued with many challenges that inhibit initiative and innovation. Nevertheless, the U.S. intelligence enterprise is likely to benefit considerably from the work going on in all of these centers, even though dialogue historically has been impeded by compartmentalization and bureaucratic politics in a declining resource environment.

Creating technical intelligence capabilities poses some unique challenges: Technical collection systems, such as imaging satellites and SIGINT platforms, typically have billion-dollar costs, including the costs of covert development, acquisition, and operation. Estimates of the investment in technical intelligence capabilities have ranged from 60 to 80 percent of a typical $30 billion dollar budget[19] for U.S. intelligence, now closer to $40 billion.[20] Technical system planning and development are especially difficult given the rapid pace of technological change, risking the waste and irrelevance of these intelligence systems as the targets they are designed to pursue evolve.

In this regard, an important intelligence collection and analysis problem involves the need to understand how adversaries undertake their own research programs. Their programs might be highly deceptive in nature, scientifically different in approach, and with fewer concerns about safety or engineering precision.[21] Finely tuned intelligence collection systems risk missing key technical clues if overly focused, or inflexible in how they collect and process information against adversaries who adopt different research models. An adversary concerned about revealing a known thermal sig-

19. See Stephen Orgett, The U.S. Intelligence Budget: A Basic Overview, CNS report for Congress, September 2004.
20. Ibid.
21. This was very much the way in which Iraq began to build WMD precursors in the early 1990s, through development paths that "violated" Western technical and economic constructs for building them.

nature associated with a known scientific process, for example, only needs to heat or chill its product to avoid intelligence collection. In other words, today's intelligence problem is no longer as simple as determining the numbers and types of Soviet aircraft. Knowing how to ferret out a chemical weapons program in a world rife with legitimate but crucial ingredients is truly a scientific challenge. And there remains a need for people who have unique technical skills, security clearances, and expertise, only a few of whom will continue to reside within the organizations of U.S. intelligence.

Basic Elements

To reiterate, while intelligence is often viewed as a walled-off enterprise, it does not and cannot operate in a vacuum: Science and technology development requires focus, investment, people, and a culture of innovation. Few of these ingredients have been richly present in U.S. intelligence over the past decade, in the period between the Cold War and the global war on terrorism. Each of these is worth examining.

Focus

Past program reviews cite "heroic leadership," the use of small teams with authority and responsibility, and an intense focus of effort as key sources of historical success in America's technical intelligence programs.[22] In recent years, however, the development of technical programs has been plagued by extensive and conflicting oversight from within both the executive and legislative branches, an overemphasis on cost control, and an exaggerated need to accumulate customer requirements as part of the process by which to

22. See Kevin Ruffimer, ed., CORONA: America's First Satellite Program, Center for the Study of Intelligence, CIA, Washington, DC, 1995, part I.

gain political and budgetary support for individual programs. Marketing, management, and political consultations have taken place at the expense of attention to the technical aspects of intelligence systems and a focus on accomplishing the specific intelligence mission. Increasing demands by intelligence consumers have also put a premium on creating near-term capabilities, vice long-term ones.[23]

Investment

As mentioned, technical intelligence systems are among the most costly aspects of the entire intelligence enterprise. Recent headlines proclaim the cost and necessity of planned technical systems.[24] The broad reduction in funding for new intelligence systems during the 1990s gave rise to a crisis of trust: The case of a new NRO facility and the "forward funding" associated with that agency ushered in a decade of detailed oversight that represented the most extensive levels of micromanagement in the history of U.S. intelligence, at least in the technical domain.[25] While the American way of planning, programming, and budgeting has its strengths, it substantially limits the flexibility of intelligence program managers in their oversight of technical programs that need to remain financially flexible and aptly funded in the face of technical, engineering, and mission challenges throughout the life cycle of their programs.

---

23. See Michael Wertheimer, "Crippling Innovation—And Intelligence," *Washington Post*, July 21, 2004, A19.

24. "New Spy Satellite Debated on Hill," *Washington Post*, December 11, 2004, A1.

25. The mid-1970s investigations into U.S. intelligence abuses of civil liberties might be a parallel basis for micromanagement, but it was less focused on technical capabilities.

People

For a variety of reasons, including mandatory personnel reductions and an expansion of lucrative opportunities in the private sector, the U.S. government experienced an overall downsizing in the early 1990s. U.S. intelligence experienced a mandatory 17 percent reduction in personnel, including a number of highly qualified technical personnel who took advantage of jobs in the communications, computing, and related industries. The end of the Cold War saw a reduced interest in American intelligence as a long-term career, because the intelligence community's importance seemed to decline and more lucrative opportunities in the private sector arose. Yet the successful exploitation of science and technology for intelligence purposes requires a highly qualified workforce with access to state-of-the-art research. Further, qualified people are not only essential to the business of building collection and analysis technical systems; in a more complex world, they are also central to the analysis of developments within it.

Culture of Innovation

Just as important as the resources associated with technical intelligence programs is the context within which they are provided and nurtured. CORONA aficionados cite the thirteen failed launches before success as emblematic of the risk that must be encouraged and accepted in order to develop truly innovative technical intelligence systems. Failure must be recognized as a legitimate part of the scientific process. While this is helpful in theory, it must also be considered in the bureaucratic and operational context of the cost of failure. Ironically, the intense oversight, limited resources, and focus on efficiency have forced intelligence program managers to a point where they avoid risk and have fewer resources—in areas like testing and systems engineering—available to optimize the chances for success for truly innovative systems.[26]

Time is of the essence. Science and technology, in general, and their specialized application to intelligence take time, but the rate of change in the world that intelligence is designed to understand is rapid. Former DCI George Tenet testified in 2001 that the "accelerating rate of change" in the world, as viewed through the eyes, ears, and brains of intelligence, was unprecedented.[27] As we now know, this rate of change has created structural weaknesses in American intelligence, such as the concentration of analysts on more tactical, day-to-day reporting. In addition, collection demands often exceed capacity, especially in global hot spots. But beyond the competition for today's collection, demands for new kinds of collection based on adversary behavior have clearly outstripped U.S. government planning, budgeting, and acquisition cycles. Even today, while the war on terror continues and new threats emerge, American intelligence is in the process of modernizing its SIGINT, IMINT, and MASINT architectures[28] for the current threat environment. Every one of the elements mentioned here—focus, investment, people, and philosophy—are keys to success in that endeavor.

Higher Level Issues and Challenges

Beyond the basic issues lie a number of other challenges to the development of technical intelligence capabilities. These include the role of priorities, needs, and requirements; internal management; external relations; research frameworks for highly risky or controversial topics; and trade-offs within the technical program.

---

26. Wertheimer, "Crippling Innovation."
27. See www.odci.gov/cia/public_affairs/speeches/2001/UNCLASWWT_0207 2001.html.
28. Various

Priorities, Needs, and Requirements

The cost of technical system planning, development, acquisition, and operations is so prohibitive that some logical link to consumer intelligence should be required. Debates have emerged in the recent past on the respective roles of functional managers for GEOINT and SIGINT (NGA and NSA) and the NRO on which overhead sensors and platforms should be built, with NGA and NSA representing intelligence consumers and NRO representing state-of-the-art knowledge of satellite platforms and technologies. Yet the effort to understand what type of information intelligence consumers say they need—in volume, type, depth, and precision—has given rise to a "tyranny of requirements" that technology developers and their managers need to deal with.

During any given data call for requirements, intelligence consumers, with no incentives to control their needs, pile on every conceivable information requirement they can imagine (and perhaps in some sense need). Rather than focusing on what intelligence can uniquely provide, consumers add thousands of information needs, stated as requirements, in the face of uncertainty about their targets and missions. The problem is compounded by the lack of a coherent system for aggregating and merging the military, intelligence, and homeland security requirements. Indeed, the problem is even worse. Today, intelligence system planning and development must be reviewed by dozens of panels and boards, the most important being the Department of Defense's Joint Requirements and Operations Council (JROC) and the CIA's Mission Requirements Board (MRB). Although these reviews serve as an important vetting process, they also have the effect of driving program managers to intense marketing of their program within the U.S. national security community. More important, these boards can impel managers to create programs that are far too complex. One consequence is that programs are canceled or scaled back—mostly on cost and technical risk concerns—to a point where they serve a "least common denominator" requirements set, often at the expense of innovation and experimentation. Among the ways to deal with these problems are to place more of the burden of proof on the consumer and to create incentives for appetite suppression among them. At the broad architectural level, efforts must be made to create a portfolio of investments, some of which provide important must-have capabilities while maintaining some innovative high-risk experiments. But experimentation must be recognized and evaluated as such, as opposed to requiring buy-in from every potential user. Real innovation is unlikely to happen without some educated risks.

Internal Management

U.S. intelligence agencies have a can-do culture that emphasizes operations and flexibility over in-depth management and planning.[29] Unlike the sets of organizations used for the Department of Defense—the Office of the Secretary of Defense and the Combatant Commands—focused on operations, and another set—the Joint Staff and the Armed Services—focused on preparing for the future, U.S. intelligence agencies maintain both functions at the agency (e.g., NSA, NGA) level. While external organizations like Congress, the Community Management Staff, and the Undersecretary of Defense for Intelligence play important roles in encouraging, scrutinizing, and overseeing these functions, in fact they are executed at the agency level. This structure has led to an unhealthy competition between operations and modernization,[30] a competition that was exacerbated by successive world crises during the 1990s. As

29. Michael Turner, *Why Secret Intelligence Fails* (Potomoc Books, 2005).

30. William Odom, *Fixing Intelligence for a More Secure America* (New Haven, CT: Yale University Press, 2004), 31–34.

intelligence demands rose, the satisfaction of them came largely at the expense of modernization across the intelligence enterprise.

While an emphasis on satisfying day-to-day intelligence needs represents one challenge to the development of technical intelligence capabilities, the culture of secrecy, a largely inadequate level of investment over the past five decades, and relative political insularity created few incentives for the development of rigorous internal management structures within the agencies. The historical lack of management data and systems and the pervasive secrecy meant that there was almost no way to determine which programs were more effective from an intelligence perspective or more cost-effective from a budget and management perspective.[31] Outside organizations, like Congress, ultimately demanded this rigor and, absent it, stepped in, perhaps dealing a blow to innovation from micromanagement.

Over time, increased oversight, the large costs associated with science and technology intelligence capabilities, the rapid pace of information technology, and other factors have created demands for better overall enterprise management. This was central to the argument for a DNI and other features of the Intelligence Reform Act. Elsewhere, normally quiet congressional concerns about how well the agencies are being managed have spilled into the public debate in the cases of the NRO[32] in the early 1990s and the NSA[33] in the more recent past; they were also a small focus of the 9/11 Commission.[34] Among the recommended elements of more rigorous management are the need to develop a strong enterprise architecture, perform better financial management, undertake more

31. David Kaplan, "Mission Impossible: The Inside Story of How a Band of Reformers Tried—and Failed—to Change America's Spy Agencies," *U.S. News and World Report*, August 2, 2004: 32–42.

32. Robert Wall and Craig Covault, "Trouble at the NRO," *U.S. News and World Report*, August 18, 2003: 24–26.

33. Wertheimer, "Crippling Innovation."

34. *The 9/11 Commission Report*.

rigorous strategic and technical planning, and develop an improved understanding of the links among requirements, investments, and outputs. Although improved internal management is an important and legitimate goal, some worry that an overemphasis on management structures removes attention from the intelligence mission and limits the potential for innovation at exactly the time when it is needed.[35] Whatever the case, intelligence managers must have a better understanding of what they are investing in, and why, especially at a time when attention to developing new capabilities is needed.

External Relations

The planning, development, acquisition, maintenance, and operations of technical systems require a strong and creative interaction with U.S. industry. This relationship historically has been an intimate one—as reflected, for example, in histories of the CIA and the NRO[36]—in part because of the nature of the work and the importance of secrecy and compartmentalization. But these old models are no longer realistic or even helpful. Changes in both government and industry have created the need for a much more open "cast of the net" to find the most potentially useful technologies. Historically, the U.S. intelligence community had access to state-of-the-art technology, by virtue of developing it (e.g., satellites and satellite processing), cultivating it as a potential source of intelligence information (e.g., telecommunications), or establishing proximity to the industry groups that were fostering innovations (e.g., computer networks). Traditional activities, like satellite programs, were large and lucrative and based on a decisive technology advantage in

35. Wertheimer, "Crippling Innovation."

36. This issue is keenly revisited in the *Studies in Intelligence* debate cited above.

space platforms, communications, satellite navigation and control, and state-of-the art exploitation systems for SIGINT and imagery.

The information age and its splintering of hardware, software, and application developers, both nationally and internationally, altered technology as well as the pace at which it changes. Today, commercial developments quickly outstrip government frameworks for understanding and acquiring capabilities in traditional ways. And as commercial opportunities expand, and the U.S. defense industry downsizes and consolidates, the challenge of knowing who to work with becomes much harder. The reduced investment levels for traditional intelligence programs during the 1990s slowed the technology investment and left almost an entire generation of industrial partners with little hands-on experience in technology or systems engineering. From a technological footrace perspective, the pressures on American intelligence were twofold, with our advantage slipping at the same time our adversaries' knowledge of them—for both their own offensive and defensive purposes—was growing.[37] Increased oversight and a demand for more accountable financial and procurement practices have exacerbated relations with U.S. industry.[38] To the extent that oversight has become more detailed, both in dollar terms as well as in technical and programmatic intent, intelligence agencies have imposed those details on the agency contractors. This constrains innovation. Rather than defining the capabilities required in broad terms and allowing the contractors to propose various technical approaches to obtain them, U.S. government agencies are tending to overspecify how the contractors should proceed.

Even if new intelligence technologies can be identified, technology insertion and systems engineering remain key gaps. Traditional acquisition approaches in government create incentives for

37. See Aris Pappas and James Simon, "The Intelligence Community, 2001–2015," in *Studies in Intelligence* (2003).
38. Wertheimer, "Crippling Innovation."

stability and longer-term architectural strategy rather than the rapid architectural changes and their attendant financial implications that today's technology and intelligence environments demand. Even if new technologies can be identified, it takes on average about ten years from the time a major technical intelligence idea is developed to the time it is used operationally, the equivalent of an ice age in the current environment. Successful transitions have involved direct user involvement in the development, the running of parallel and redundant capabilities, and the determination tolerance for failure. Many of these are very difficult to achieve in intelligence, given technical system complexity, the cost of redundancy, and the need to deliver must-have capability to the intelligence mission. These realities are forcing decisions that may create near-term capabilities, but ones that may come at the expense of longer-term intelligence advantages.

To summarize, the state of relations between the intelligence community and U.S. industry today involves too many structural barriers and intellectual boundaries, including ingrained expectations about procedures and oversight mechanisms. Technical systems are no longer conceived and built in an environment structured to sustain an innovative spirit. Rather, they emerge from a consensus-based process designed to satisfy as many standardized engineering and financial requirements as possible. Planning occurs from the top down, rather than from the bottom up. Systems integration, which should derive from technological best practices, has become a political and actuarial process that values integration *within* agencies at the expense of integration *across* agencies. This runs contrary to the direction in which American intelligence should be headed.[39]

Ineffective use of the commercial sector is a particularly serious problem. Intelligence technologies for collection and analysis range

---

39. Taken from O'Connell and Tomes, "Keeping the Information Edge."

from the one-of-a-kind, exotic systems—such as satellites or SIGINT collectors—to the kinds of collaborative networked environments that both professionals and even students have grown accustomed to in their work. While intelligence technologies have been historically developed and built within the government or its first-tier vetted industry partners, there are increasing opportunities, even in the systems realm, to make use of emerging technologies from the commercial sector. But how and when to use commercial technologies and practices remain hotly contested questions. Although government acquisition usually ensures a capability tailored to specific requirements—using known providers and under known security conditions—costs are generally higher in government procurement. Using commercial technologies usually requires less funding, but also less control of the process and the overall market.

Of course, the private sector today is often more effective at providing information technology and services than is the government. This was reflected in the highly successful establishment by the CIA of In-Q-Tel, a nonprofit venture capital fund designed to connect with entrepreneurs, established companies, universities, researchers, and venture capitalists in order to develop technologies—mostly information technologies—that provide superior intelligence capabilities.[40] The In-Q-Tel model has been so successful—more than sixty investments in companies whose technologies help improve intelligence processing and analysis—that U.S. intelligence and even other government managers have tried to expand and export the model, which relies heavily on the DCI's special acquisition authorities.[41]

But what about the areas of technical intelligence beyond information technology, such as those required to gather exotic signals or the development of WMD? Clearly, the government-industry mix

40. See In-Q-tel website at www.in-q-it.com.
41. Interview with Gilman Louie, "Defense Firms Look to Mimic CIA Strategic Venture Firm," *Federal News*, July 12, 2004: 8.

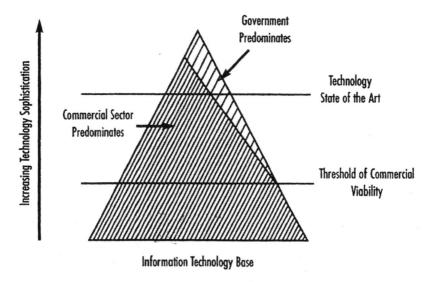

Relationship and Comparative Advantages of Government and Commercial Technology Sectors

will be different, based on current investment levels and market demands. One approach is to have the government take maximal advantage of the commercial sector while continuing to emphasize its own investments in areas where no market is desirable or expected to emerge. The chart, from Bruce Berkowitz, depicts the comparative advantages that government and industry have in regard to technology.

The government's role is much smaller overall than that of the private sector, but it is concentrated at the more advanced levels.[42] This reflects the realities on both sides of the fence, namely, that the government has more of an ability to spend money without regard to a bottom line—in essence, taking more risk—while industry is much more sensitive to the bottom line. Industry is therefore available for capabilities that are important, but perhaps less state-

42. The argument of this section is drawn from Bruce Berkowitz and Melvin Goodman, *Best Truth: Intelligence in the Information Age* (New Haven, CT: Yale University Press, 2002), ch. 2.

of-the art, absent government guarantees and investment. Berkowitz describes a number of possible approaches to exploiting the private sector for intelligence purposes, including subsidization and partial privatization, flexible regulation, and the creation of competition within the government. While each of these approaches has been pursued, the last is typically hindered by traditional secrecy and mission specialization, as well as a culture that has tried to eliminate competition for both good and bad reasons.

There is good news. Some innovative approaches have been tried to some success. Each year, the NRO director's Innovation Initiative casts a very wide net concerning the future of the space reconnaissance enterprise and the technologies that might help transform it.[43] This initiative has been creative not only in terms of its role in advancing the NRO's mission, but also in feeding other intelligence community agencies with potentially innovative ideas. CIA's STEP program, undertaken by the Directorate of Science and Technology, fosters links to scientists, researchers, and technologists in academia and industry for purposes of providing inputs to key analytic and technical questions underpinning U.S. intelligence. And, in the past, a broad exchange between the intelligence community and environmental scientists fostered as much of a benefit for U.S. intelligence as it did for improving how we might understand key collection and analysis questions related to the environment.[44] In all cases, this broader network of collaborations with academia and industry has pointed to a key method for advancing the use of science and technology for intelligence purposes.

43. DII website at www.nro.gov.
44. See Kevin O'Connell, *Using Intelligence Data for Environmental Needs: Balancing National Objectives* (RAND, 1996).

Trade-offs

As intelligence managers exploit science and technology for the purposes of improving intelligence, they must understand the trade-offs they are making within their programs and, ultimately, within the entire architecture. As mentioned, American intelligence has devoted an inordinate amount of resources and attention to the collection of data, rather than to its processing and exploitation. Collection that remains unexploited—lacking analysis and contextual consideration—may be as useless as no collection at all. Security practices must shift toward allowing better intelligence sharing, and even the most secretive project today must be planned with a view toward the day when it is less secret or even known in a widespread fashion. In this newfound intelligence-sharing environment, managers will have to realize, like Silicon Valley did, that advantage is fleeting. Maintaining the intelligence edge will require much shorter cycles of innovation.

Understanding trade-offs is important in other ways, such as the drive for greater efficiency across the entire intelligence enterprise. Congress, for example, has strongly criticized the poor coordination of and trade-off analysis within intelligence investment in potentially redundant capabilities like UAVs and satellites.[45] While efficiency is rarely a useful goal in the collection of intelligence, it must remain an important target for resource use and allocation. Scale and scalability of new technical concepts must also be understood: Technological innovations may mean nothing without parallel adaptations in both organizations and people. While an extraordinary amount of work has gone into developing analyst tools, these are typically disregarded by analysts unless they are easy to learn, easy to use, and increase the amount of time that they have to think.[46] And while some technology-driven develop-

45. See Best, *Intelligence, Surveillance, and Reconnaissance Programs.*
46. RAND Analytic Tradecraft report (forthcoming).

ments are extremely positive, producing highly innovative intelligence under tight and operationally challenging time lines, uncertainty remains about where these activities actually fit within the overall intelligence enterprise.

V. MOVING AHEAD WITH SCIENCE AND TECHNOLOGY

The global war on terrorism, WMD proliferation, and other intelligence challenges demand a complex approach to understanding our adversaries, including their capabilities, their potential to change, and, most important, their intentions. While the post-9/11 public discussion about the future of U.S. intelligence has been fraught with gross generalizations—such as "less TECHINT, more HUMINT"[47]—the reality is that we must use each part of our intelligence enterprise to maximum effect and in as creative and synergistic a way as possible.

Long a key element in the American intelligence arsenal, science and technology will continue to play a crucial role for U.S. intelligence, whether in creating new capabilities or in improving our ability to use existing ones. But it will have to do so in a much more difficult context than in the past, to deal with the dual challenges of increased complexity in the intelligence mission and of changing balances in the use of technology. In a period of increased transparency and intelligence footraces, U.S. intelligence will have to get beyond moving faster and more efficiently; it must become qualitatively more effective in collecting, processing, disseminating, and acting upon information. In a rapidly changing information market, U.S. intelligence innovations must drive toward increasingly specific and specialized forms of information. And identifying and breaking sanctuary for our adversaries will have to become the new norm for U.S. intelligence. Moving from a target-based orien-

---

47. See Bruce D. Berkowitz and Alan Goodman, *Best Truth: Intelligence in the Information Age* (New Haven, CT: Yale University Press, 2000), 41.

tation to more of a search orientation will have to take place as well.

Science and technology can dramatically improve U.S. intelligence in a world of greater threat and greater transparency. They must provide new and exotic sources of information in addition to the daily information commodities—basic images, intercepts, and technical reports that help us understand the "normal" state of the world. These new sources will help us maintain an information advantage. In a world of information overload and opportunity, science and technology must also help optimize our most important intelligence resource—people—by optimizing the targets, issues, and details on which these people focus.

We can optimize the utility of technology by a renewed concentration on management of all the key elements—risk, resources, and people—that underpin the development of new technical capabilities. And by managing the elements not only inside our intelligence organizations—for better and worse, the locus of preparation for the future—but also within the U.S. industrial base and other outsiders who can bring creative new approaches, new ideas, and expertise to bear on the future of the intelligence enterprise.

The key to success in the intelligence footrace is a renewed emphasis on innovation across the intelligence spectrum.[48] Real innovations alter core tasks—an extremely difficult undertaking for centralized, insular intelligence organizations that persist more as self-protective guilds than as the complex adaptive organizations that are required to anticipate and respond to rational, strategic adversaries engaging in asymmetric attacks. These adversaries are rational in that they learn, adapt, and organize based on our defenses. And they are strategic because they have long-term objectives and engage in planning to meet them by adjusting to our actions, capabilities, and knowledge about the strategic environ-

---

48. Taken from O'Connell and Tomes, "Keeping the Information Edge."

ment. Sustaining America's information edge is less about infrastructure than it is about leadership, engendering cultural change, encouraging entrepreneurial analysis, and learning to accept risk, whether in operational, informational, or acquisition processes. It requires focus and innovation at every level, with an active public debate about the strategic effectiveness and future direction of U.S. intelligence.

Finally, there is a need to nurture and reinvigorate the intelligence community's innovation ethos—to reenergize and focus American ingenuity on emerging intelligence collection, analysis, counterintelligence, and other challenges. Doing so, in past eras, has advanced both our leadership in world affairs and our ability to prevent conflicts or terrorist attacks at home and abroad. The global war on terrorism and the broader U.S. national security environment provide a context that is ripe for pursuing intelligence innovations across American intelligence. Within the current storm clouds over U.S. intelligence is a consensus for change, including innovation and experimentation. To maintain our intelligence advantage, we must take advantage of it.

Index